BAYO ONIYE
REALITY
of
Grace

Life-Transforming Devotional for Everyday Living

Unless otherwise indicated, all Scripture quotations are taken from the *Holy Bible, New International Version*®. NIV®. Copyright © 1973, 1978, 1984, 2011 by Biblica, Inc. Used by permission of Zondervan Publishing House. All rights reserved worldwide. (www.Zondervan.com)

Scripture quotations marked (KJV) are taken from the *King James Version* of the Bible.

Scripture quotations marked (AMP) are taken from *The Amplified Bible* (AMP).
Copyright © 1954, 1958, 1962, 1964, 1965, 1987 by The Lockman Foundation. Used by permission.

Reality of Grace
Life-Transforming Devotional for Everyday Living

ISBN 978-0-9934634-0-2
© Copyright Bayo Oniye, 2015
Bayo Oniye Resources
www.realityofgrace.org

Published by Bayo Oniye Resources
Printed in the United Kingdom
First Edition, first print: November 2015

All rights reserved. This book or any portion thereof may not be reproduced or used in any manner whatsoever without the express written permission of the publisher.

DEDICATION

This book is dedicated to my loving son, Joseph Rafiwa Oniye. You can't come to us but we will see you one day. Sleep well!

To my loving wife, Bakang. I am so blessed with you in my life. You are worth more than rubies and diamonds. Together we are coheirs of the grace of life.

Neo and Joshua, what a privilege it is to serve you as Daddy, I am indeed blessed!

To my dearest Mum, Rebecca. Thank you for your love, support and words of encouragement.

TABLE OF CONTENTS

Dedication 3
Acknowledgements 7
Chapter 1: This is your moment 8
Chapter 2: Abraham's blessings are mine 11
Chapter 3: Ever fresh, ever green 14
Chapter 4: World Book Day 17
Chapter 5: Jesus is enough 21
Chapter 6: Birds fly, dogs bark, believers believe 24
Chapter 7: Let Daddy fix it 28
Chapter 8: His resurrection is proof of my justification 31
Chapter 9: We are acceptable to God 35
Chapter 10: God helps those who believe Him 38
Chapter 11: All things are working together for our good .. 43
Chapter 12: Shouts of 'Grace, Grace' 47
Chapter 13: Complete in Him, lacking nothing 52
Chapter 14: The substance of my affection 55
Chapter 15: The sufficiency of grace 59
Chapter 16: His finished work is our resting ground 62
Chapter 17: The uplifting power of grace 65
Chapter 18: Redeemed from sickness 68
Chapter 19: God is a happy God 73
Chapter 20: The new covenant is better 77

Chapter 21: One Thing 83
Chapter 22: You look amazing under the light 88
Chapter 23: God never leaves you in limbo 91
Chapter 24: Add value to your life 94
Chapter 25: His presence makes the difference 97
Chapter 26: God is not put off by our sin 100
Chapter 27: Accessing the promises of God 103
Chapter 28: Grace management 106
Chapter 29: Enjoy good health 109
Chapter 30: Milk versus meat 112
Chapter 31: Grace-directed activity 115
Chapter 32: Astronomical progress 118
Chapter 33: Anointed with oil 121
Chapter 34: Pull out your receipt 125
Chapter 35: You've been upgraded to first class 128
Chapter 36: Looking for a job? 131
Chapter 37: It's my time of grace and favour 135
Chapter 38: Made in His image 138
Chapter 39: He is never too late 141
Chapter 40: You're the real deal – the genuine article 144
Chapter 41: Nothing is as big as our God 148
Chapter 42: Death is reversed 150
Chapter 43: Favour finds me 154
Chapter 44: Embrace the new and live a purpose-filled life ... 157
Chapter 45: Most precious to me 161
Chapter 46: The hand of the Lord 164
Chapter 47: Under pressure we don't come unglued 167
Chapter 48: We can't, but He can 170
Chapter 49: Where does it itch? 174

Chapter 50: Free grace 177
Chapter 51: Perfect peace 180
Chapter 52: Receiving the call to grace 185
Closing Words 189

Acknowledgements

I would like to give Jesus the highest praise and boast about His love for me. What an honour and privilege to be a member of His body.

Many thanks to all my teachers, mentors and pastors. It's been an honour serving and receiving from you. I am walking on the shoulders of giants who have forged the way ahead for me.

Also to the members of the four churches my wife and I have had the honour of pastoring. Thank you for receiving us and serving the purpose of God together in our generation.

Chapter 1:
This is your moment

See, I am doing a new thing! Now it springs up; do you not perceive it? I am making a way in the wilderness and streams in the wasteland.

Isaiah 43:19

Do you feel uncomfortable with where you are? Do you feel that your support system and the structures you once depended on are now becoming a distant memory? Do you feel alone in a strange land, where things you were once accustomed to are no more? Well don't be discouraged, because you are just about to break new ground. Sometimes sudden changes, shifts and shake-ups in our lives are precursors to the amazing work God wants to establish.

At certain points in our lives, we get so accustomed to our old ways that it becomes difficult to let go and embrace the new. It is like teaching a dog a new trick.

For forty years the children of Israel were in the wilderness, they were accustomed to eating bread and meat – the manna and quail God provided from heaven. Several generations fed sumptuously on this heavenly prepared meal, until they got to the Promised Land. The supply of manna was cut off as soon as they reached the border of Canaan.

No more manna didn't mean God had deserted them. An end to the supply of this provision did not mean they had grievously sinned against God. The end of the supply marked the beginning of a new dawn. This was an indication that they had arrived in the land God had promised them. It must have been a weird feeling for them to go out in the morning and expect their daily supply, only to find nothing. Perhaps the children went back into their tents and said to their parents 'there is no manna today', sparking questions about what they were going to eat.

> *The Israelites ate manna forty years, until they came to a land that was settled; they ate manna until they reached the border of Canaan.*
> **Exodus 16:35**

God cut off the supply because the season of their lives had just changed. In the wilderness, they were not adapted to feeding on any other type of meal. Canaan was completely different. It was a land that flowed with milk and honey. It was a land filled with vineyards and olive trees. A land replete with corn, wine and oil. They had just entered into the best time of their lives.

You may have just lost a job or a business deal. People you trusted may have left you in the lurch. Don't be discouraged:

God is setting you up for a new season. Your best days have just begun. You are in for a treat: the never-ending supply of God's grace. Stay focused. You cannot use the tools that supported you in the wilderness in this new land God has brought you into. Thank God for the manna of the wilderness but move on to eat of the good in the land. God is doing a new thing in your life. This is your moment. It's your time!!

PRAYER

Thank You, Father, for taking me to higher grounds. Thank You for opening doors no man can shut and for closing doors that are not good for me. In all things, I trust You and even though I don't fully understand the season I'm in, You will cause all things to work for my highest good.

Chapter 2:

Abraham's Blessings Are Mine

He redeemed us in order that the blessing given to Abraham might come to the Gentiles through Christ Jesus, so that by faith we might receive the promise of the Spirit.
Galatians 3:14

When the Lord first appeared to Abraham (Abram), He asked him to leave his family and go to a land God was to show him. God immediately began to make unconditional promises to Abraham. He said 'I will make you into a great nation, and I will bless you; I will make your name great, and you will be a blessing. I will bless those who bless you, and whoever curses you I will curse; and all peoples on earth will be blessed through you' (Genesis 12:2–3). What did Abraham do to deserve all these promises? Nothing. Abraham did nothing for God to make the promises. It was an unconditional promise completely dependent on God for its fulfilment. It is also interesting to note that one of the translations for the word 'blessing' is 'gift'. So God said to Abraham, 'I will bless you, I will make your name great and you will be a gift.'

A gift is usually given freely and unconditionally. It is given to express the heart, love and generosity of the giver towards the recipient. God made all these promises to Abraham to show His heart, love, generosity and irrevocable goodness towards Abraham. In making Abraham such promises, God includes all people of the earth as participants in, or benefactors of, the blessing. I am reminded of an old song that includes the lyrics, 'Abraham's blessings are mine, Abraham's blessings are mine, I am blessed in the morning, blessed in the evening, Abraham's blessings are mine'.

Abraham received and walked in all the blessings God had for him by believing God. Abraham did not have to perform or try to impress God. As Abraham walked with God, God gave him a picture of how blessed he would be by showing him the innumerable stars of the sky. After God preached to him the gospel using the visual aid of the stars in the sky, Abram believed the Lord, and He credited it to him as righteousness (Genesis 15:6).

Abraham was convinced that the blessing was his to the point of believing God. When God saw Abraham's faith, God said he was righteous for believing Him. Today's questions are 'Are we blessed with Abraham's blessing? Do we have what Abraham had?' The answer is a resounding 'YES!' Through Jesus Christ, we have the blessing of Abraham. The same way the fulfilment of Abraham's blessing came about is the same way we receive the blessings of Abraham today. It was independent of Abraham: it was an unconditional blessing and depended fully on God. Today we are blessed with the blessings of Abraham as a gift – not earned, but believed and received. It is God's gift to us, and the greatest honour we can show the giver of a gift is to receive His gift and not try to earn it. Abraham believed God and walked in the manifestation of the blessing. We believe God and today we are blessed with Abraham's blessing.

PRAYER

Dear Jesus, thank You for Your unconditional love for me. You loved me even when I was a sinner. Today it is Your unconditional love that causes me to partake of the blessing. I am blessed with Abraham's blessings, all because of You.

CHAPTER 3:

EVER FRESH, EVER GREEN

The righteous will flourish like a palm tree, they will grow like a cedar of Lebanon; planted in the house of the Lord, they will flourish in the courts of our God. They will still bear fruit in old age, they will stay fresh and green, proclaiming, "The Lord is upright; he is my Rock, and there is no wickedness in him."
Psalm 92:12–15

The shelf life of commodities varies, depending on their type and quality. For example, a banana may have a shelf life of two weeks, while a tin of beans may have one of two years. One thing is certain that after the shelf life on any product is passed, the quality is no longer guaranteed and the product may be unfit for use or consumption.

When the Lord provided for His children in the wilderness, God instructed them, through Moses, on how to receive His provision. They were required to gather just enough. They were also required not to keep any for the next day. God intended to provide a fresh supply of manna every day. The instruction was not followed by the children of Israel: some kept the manna until the following morning. The same manna that once brought nutrition to their bodies now bred maggots and began to stink. They showed, through their actions, that they doubted God's ability to cater for them daily. Instead, they trusted in their ability to hold on to what they had, and this attempt at self-sufficiency proved futile.

> *The Israelites did as they were told; some gathered much, some little. And when they measured it by the omer, the one who gathered much did not have too much, and the one who gathered little did not have too little. Everyone had gathered just as much as they needed. Then Moses said to them, "No one is to keep any of it until morning." However, some of them paid no attention to Moses; they kept part of it until morning, but it was full of maggots and began to smell. So Moses was angry with them.*
>
> **Exodus 16:17–20**

Later, they got the message and trusted in God's ability to supply their needs every day. God then commanded them to take some of the manna and keep it for generations to come. How were they to preserve a food with a shelf life of less than 24 hours for several decades? There were no refrigerators or food preservatives in the wilderness. There were no canning systems or electric dehydrators to dry their food, but God told them what to do. He told them to put a measure of the manna in a jar and then place the jar before the Lord in the Ark of the Covenant.

God was teaching them a vital lesson here. The manna in the hands of humans will decay and breed worms, but in the presence of God it stays fresh.

Do you feel worn out? Do you feel like you are almost past your 'best before' date, with your strength failing and sharpness fading? You have waited so long and now have no strength to go the extra mile. The key to staying ever fresh is to stay in the presence of God. Put your life into His hands and everything about you will be preserved. In fact, here lies the key to growing gracefully: putting your life in God's hands.

PRAYER

Heavenly Father, thank You for taking care of me. I know You have a fresh supply for my daily needs. I am not worried about what tomorrow may bring because You know my tomorrow. I place every area of my life into Your hands. My education, business, health, family, work, finances, everything. I trust you. I am refreshed in Your presence. I am renewed by Your grace.

CHAPTER 4:

WORLD BOOK DAY

Therefore, there is now no condemnation for those who are in Christ Jesus.

Romans 8:1

As the rigorous schedule of my week became more demanding, my little boy reminded me about his school's participation in World Book Day. He had told me several days before that everyone in his reception class was to dress up as a character from their favourite book. That week was eventful for us as parents, with a lot of travelling, and we only happened to remember Joshua's costume the night before it was needed. It was just too late to do anything about it. The following morning, while getting Joshua ready for school, He asked 'Daddy, why am I wearing my school uniform?' and continued, 'I should be dressed as a Gruffalo.' I bit my tongue because I simply had no answer to his question.

I got him to school that morning and almost everyone else was in their fancy costumes. Turning to my little boy, as tears rolled down his face, I said 'Daddy is really sorry. Next time we'll get you a Gruffalo *and* a Spider-Man costume.'

After dropping him off at school, I walked back to the car, and a sense of guilt and condemnation clouded my mind. Within a few minutes, a deluge of thoughts concerning my ability to be a good father filled my head. These were just a few thoughts that came to mind that day:

'You are too busy running around for everyone, yet you don't care about your son.'

'You pastor a church and yet you can't even get your son a simple costume for this day.'

'How many World Book Days have you got in a year? The only opportunity you had was blown up by your so-called busy schedule. You are not a good father. What about his mother? What was she doing all the time he mentioned this day?'

I reached my pocket for my mobile phone and called my wife. Over the phone, I expressed my frustration. These were a few questions I asked her too.

Did you not know it's World Book Day today? Why did you not check Joshua's bag before leaving the house? We are both parents and just because I am dropping him off at school does not mean I should be responsible for looking into his bag to see what is required all of the time. On and on the questions went down the phone at my lovely wife who was – as always – so gracious to me.

I hung up the phone and my day almost went into a downward spiral of negative thoughts. I was feeling condemned for not being a caring and loving father. Then I remembered a message I listened to on guilt and condemnation by Pastor Prince. He said something along the lines of 'If you don't accept the devil's condemnation, he cannot steal from you.' As soon as that thought came to mind, I snapped out of the dungeon of depressing thought and told God how sorry I was for feeling condemned about myself.

That day after school, something happened that had never happened in all of Joshua's time at school. When I picked him up, he had the biggest smile on his face and shouted 'Daddy, look at the board!' I looked up towards the board and to my greatest surprise he was amongst a few other kids who were the top of their class that day. Joshua had never achieved this before, but for the first time he did it on the same day I thought I had made a huge mistake. God just put the biggest smile on my face. I knew it was God trying to say something. There is no condemnation because we are in Christ Jesus.

You may feel you have not done something completely right and you may be beating yourself up because you feel inadequate to meet an expectation. Friend, don't allow the feeling of guilt and condemnation into your heart. Instead, focus on other things that God has done through you and for you. When guilt and condemnation set in, Satan uses them as a foothold to ruin your day and whole week. So don't allow him. We may feel insufficient but our sufficiency is of Christ and in Him we are complete.

PRAYER

Thank You, Abba Father, for Jesus. Because of Jesus, I will not walk in guilt and condemnation. I let go of past mistakes and regrets and today I receive all the grace You have for me. It's a new day.

CHAPTER 5:

JESUS IS ENOUGH

However, to the one who does not work but trusts God who justifies the ungodly, their faith is credited as righteousness.
Romans 4:5

Every legal justice system has a dual commitment to punish the guilty and acquit the innocent, so when we think of God as a just and righteous Judge, the question often arises: 'If God is a just God, how can He justify the sinner?'

The answer to this question is rooted in the cross of Calvary. The cross is the righteous foundation through which the sinner or guilty one is justly acquitted.

Let's say you go shopping for some groceries at your local grocery store. You select all the items you have on your shopping list and tick the list as you go along. After shopping, when you go to the till and make payment for your groceries, you are presented with a receipt that shows all the items you bought. On getting home, while you make yourself a cup of tea, you peruse the items on the receipt to make sure nothing was left out.

Whilst going through the list, you realise there is a double entry for a bag of potatoes. You were charged for two bags instead of one. What will you do after realising you have been charged twice for a single item you bought? I dare say a few people will overlook the error and decide not to rectify it. Others may not even be aware as they may not care less about keeping the receipt, let alone go through it. However, a few people will go back to the store, tell them about the mistake and request a refund. A good store will refund you for their error and may even give you extra as a goodwill gesture. You only pay for what you buy!

On the cross of Calvary, our Lord Jesus paid for the punishment of our sins. He was punished on our account. All our sins were paid for on the cross. He paid the debt to redeem us. The debt that brings us forgiveness of sins, healing in our body and soundness of mind was all paid, once and for all, on the cross.

Satan's plan today is to get the believer to think they have to pay again for their sins. He convinces people that sickness and disease are the punishments God gives as a retribution for our sins. My friend, Jesus paid for it once and for all and you don't have to pay again. God requires no payment from us, because His Son paid it all.

God is righteous and righteousness demands that sin is punished. When Jesus hung on the cross, He took upon His body the punishment for our sins. All of our sins were paid for as Jesus hung on the cross.

The only payment that could completely emancipate us from the bondage of sin and our inability to meet the demands of the Law was the precious blood of Jesus. Now that the price has been paid once and for all, the justice of God is now on our side. Today, God is righteous not to demand from us a payment that has already been made by Jesus.

Just as it is not OK for you to pay twice for a single item, the righteousness of God demands that the sinner who puts their trust in Jesus is not only justified but receives the free gift of righteousness. God will not punish you again for the same sin our Lord Jesus paid for on the cross. So when Satan tries to convince you to accept sickness as a payment or punishment for a sin you commit, you can boldly declare 'I've been paid for and the blood of Jesus is enough payment for the wholeness and well-being of my life.'

PRAYER
Thank you Father because today, I have the gift of righteousness and I am redeemed. The price that paid for my redemption also brought about my wholeness. Jesus paid it all on the cross for me and by faith I am justified and forgiven forever. Jesus is enough.

CHAPTER 6:

BIRDS FLY, DOGS BARK, BELIEVERS BELIEVE

Do not offer any part of yourself to sin as an instrument of wickedness, but rather offer yourselves to God as those who have been brought from death to life; and offer every part of yourself to him as an instrument of righteousness. For sin shall no longer be your master, because you are not under the law, but under grace.

Romans 6:13–14

A bird can fly because the ability to fly is coded in its very nature. Its DNA has the code to fly. Fish swim for the same reason. The ability to thrive in an aquatic habitat is inherent in their nature. Just as water is to a fish, so is air to a bird.

Both are active living and thriving creatures with differing abilities, designed and made by God. A kingfisher dives into the water for a few seconds and comes out with its prey in its beak. A photograph of the bird at this moment may show it to be completely immersed. However, just because the bird is in water for a few seconds does not make it a fish. The bird has not got the coding of a fish to live in water. Equally, a flying fish may occasionally fly out of the water to escape a predator, but then returns to the water because the nature of fish is to live in water. It will never be found perching in a tree or tweeting like a bird.

As believers, our very nature changed the day we accepted Jesus as Lord and Saviour. That same day, we were coded with the nature of God. We received the gift of righteousness and became the righteousness of God in Christ. Along the way in our walk with God, it is possible for the believer to sin. However, once you are a believer, sin does not redefine your nature. As a believer, it is impossible for your nature to be that of a sinner.

A dog may run into a pond but will not stay there. The dog will eventually either find its way out or be rescued by its owner. When a duck gets into a pond it thrives there. The duck enjoys the water and loves living there.

These analogies give an explanation to who you are as a believer. Before we got saved, our nature was sin. We all inherited the sin nature from the first man, Adam, but when we were saved we took on a whole new nature. Our identity changed. Now we have the nature to live righteously and enjoy righteousness. Sometimes along the way, we may fall into sin just like a dog may fall into the pond. In there, our nature remains unchanged by the circumstance or by what brought about the sin. We are still the righteousness of God in Christ.

Believers who fall into sin genuinely feel bad and remorseful because they know that is not their nature. They are aware of who they are and immediately agree with God that their sins has already been forgiven through the atoning sacrifice of Jesus Christ. To this end, they confess their righteous stance before God. Anyone who lives in sin, enjoys it and practises it while professing to be a believer is a highly deluded individual.

When you are deeply in love with someone, the last thing on your mind will be devising a means to hurt them. You want to do everything to show them how much you love them, to preserve the good in the relationship. A believer madly in love with God is not looking for a way to sin or to displease Him. The grace of God in us teaches us how to live godly lives. When you miss the mark as a believer, instead of wallowing in the decadence of sin in your life, focus on who Christ made you. Don't focus on the old nature of sin, which is crucified with Christ; focus on the new creation, the new nature that is alive forever. Be more conscious of who you are in Christ as the righteousness of God.

Paul said in Romans 8:1: 'There is no more condemnation to those who are in Christ Jesus.' Satan's plan is to always get a believer to operate as if under the law. He does this by keeping them focused on themselves. When you are focused on yourself, you also focus on your inadequacies and limitations. Condemnation arises when the self cannot measure up. Once you feel guilty and condemned, the devil has got you. Instead of focusing on yourself, focus on Christ, because through him we are complete, we measure up to God's standards and lack in no area. We have the very nature of Christ in us.

Friend, say no to condemnation, no to guilt and step into the liberty and freedom that Jesus Christ died to give you. You are the righteousness of God in Christ.

PRAYER

Thank You, Father, that I am the righteousness of God in Christ: my nature has changed. I am not a sinner, I am saved by grace. The grace of God gives me victory over sin. I live not under the Law but under grace. And so today, because of Jesus, I am well pleasing to the Father. All my deeds, thoughts and actions are righteous by faith.

Chapter 7:

Let Daddy Fix It

Praise be to the Lord, to God our Saviour, who daily bears our burdens.

Psalm 68:19

Every day, God has something amazing and awesome for His children. As a good Father, He is never caught unaware of our needs, or the demands life places on our shoulders. As a father, He understands you intimately and knows what you can do with or without. In 1 Corinthians 10:13, Paul says God will not allow us to go through what we cannot handle and will always provide us with a door of escape.

You may feel inundated with the demands of life. You might have a child who needs special care and attention or a pending deadline to meet. It could be a long-term goal you have set yourself to achieve within a specific time and you feel burdened by the pressures vying for your attention. Here is good news: God's grace is sufficient for you to do all that is required. You will not crumble under pressure, because our Father cares for us and bears all our burdens. 'Cast all your anxiety on him because he cares for you' (1 Peter 5:7).

I imagine you are sitting to read this devotional. Before sitting down, you probably did not give a conscious thought to sitting down. You did not check the strength of the chair or its ability to hold your weight, but just pulled the chair out to sit on without thinking. You put your trust in the ability of the chair to hold you and never doubted. You did not question the chair's ability to perform its duty in supporting you. You just sat! So it is with our heavenly Father. He is our burden bearer and has the ability to hold us together even when life seems to pull us apart. Just as we trusted the chair, not questioning its ability to hold us up, our heavenly Father wants us to put our trust and confidence in Him. Sit down, rest in His grace and let Him carry your burdens.

You are not at your best when burdened down by the weights of life. Certainly your shoulders are not designed to carry the burdens of the world. A mind cluttered with worry and stress has no room to receive the life-changing benefits God has for us. The blessings and benefits of God are best received when a heart is free from the clutter of worry and stress.

Jesus, in responding to his disciples' question about who will be the greatest in the kingdom of heaven, said, 'Truly I tell you, unless you change and become like little children, you will never enter the kingdom of heaven' (Matthew 18:3). I used to wonder why He made reference to children. The answer became clear when my son Joshua was born.

Joshua never worries about what to eat, what to drink or what to wear after school. As a baby he never worried about his nappy being changed or his food being prepared. Daddy and Mummy were always responsible (and still are). All he needed to do was just ask: 'Daddy, I am hungry'; 'Mummy, I am thirsty'. When Joshua needs anything, he just asks and it is the delight of his parents to meet his needs. One day, his toy broke and after many futile attempts to fix it himself, he remembered, 'Daddy can fix this'.

He stayed up late until I got home from work and the first thing he said was 'Daddy, fix this!' I put down my bag and got fixing. That night, I got an overwhelming sense of joy and accomplishment as I fixed my son's toy. The joy came from Joshua's confidence in my ability to fix his toy.

God is delighted when we assume the place of child and allow Him to assume the place of father. He loves you, He can fix it, He can provide for all your needs and surely can take good care of you. Cast your care on Him. Trust Him and see His unmerited favour, blessing and benefits flow into your life.

PRAYER

Heavenly Father, I cast my cares on You, knowing that You care for me. I am Your child and You are my Father. I put my day into Your hands. I trust You and know Your grace is sufficient for me today. I thank You for bearing me up in every situation. Today I receive all the benefits You have prepared for me.

Chapter 8:

His Resurrection is Proof of My Justification

He was delivered over to death for our sins and was raised to life for our justification.

Romans 4:25

Every year on Easter Day, we celebrate the greatest season in history: the death, burial and resurrection of our Lord and Saviour, Jesus Christ.

Romans 4:25 tells us why Jesus died on the cross and why He was raised from the dead: '[He] was delivered for our offences, and was raised again for our justification.'

On the cross, God treated Jesus like a sin offering. He who knew no sin was made sin for us. God credited to His account the sins of the whole world, from the time of Adam until the day He returns. All of our sins, past, present and future, were laid upon Jesus. Jesus bore the brunt of God's wrath because as a holy God, sin can never go unpunished – the holiness of God demands that the price for sin must be paid. However, instead of you and me paying for our sins, which we could never have done because of our very sinful nature, God sent His only Son Jesus as a man to redeem us from our sins. Jesus became our substitute on the cross and paid the price that we could never have paid, to meet the holy and righteous demands of God.

On the cross, the judgement for our sins was executed on the body of Jesus. Our substitute, Jesus Christ, took our place on the cross. His body became the lightning rod that attracted all of God's anger and indignation at our sins (John 12:32). For three hours, the sun was swallowed up in darkness. The ever-cherished Father-Son relationship was momentarily suspended, replaced by a righteous God and a sacrificial victim. On the cross, for the first time, Jesus called his Father 'God'. There He took our place as He wilfully surrendered His life to the Father's will. He completely exhausted every iota of God's wrath on the cross.

After the penalty was paid in full, Jesus was raised up from the dead on account of our justification. Friend, have you ever wondered why Jesus was raised from the dead? Some say 'He was raised from the dead because He is the Son of God'. Well, He has always been God's Son. He was raised from the dead because He did a perfect work of putting away our sins once and for all.

Paul implies in Romans 4:25 that if we are not justified, through the death of Jesus on the cross, then Jesus would not have been raised from the dead. If there were the tiniest sin lingering unpunished on the body of Jesus, He would not have been raised from the dead. The resurrection of Jesus is a public show and declaration of God that Jesus paid the price for our sins in full on the cross. Because of this perfect work, whoever believes in Jesus is justified forever.[1]

He was treated like the worst sinner on the cross because of us, so that today we can be treated as the righteousness of God in Christ. He was rejected on the cross so that today you and I can forever be accepted. He was afflicted so that we don't have to be. His body was broken so ours can be made whole. He was spat on so we don't have to be ashamed. A crown of thorns was beaten continuously into His head (see Mark 15:17–19) so that the crown of God's blessing can rest permanently on ours. Long nails were driven into His hands so that you can do right deeds with yours. His legs were nailed to the cross so that you can walk upright and righteously with yours. His heart ruptured at the thrust of the soldier's spear so our hearts would never be broken with grief, pain or affliction from Satan. His rejection, which lasted for a moment on the cross, is our acceptance forever before a holy God when we believe. Today, we can walk with our heads up high, with no regrets or shame from the past, because Jesus took our shame on the cross. He was beaten so we don't have to be sick and by His stripes we are healed (Isaiah 53:3–5). His resurrection is proof of our justification. God is a just God and we are completely forgiven on the basis of His justice. Jesus was

---

[1] Joseph Prince, *His resurrection, my justification* (CD Sermon), 8 April 2012. Singapore: Joseph Prince Resources.

punished on our account and because God is righteous, He completely forgives those who put their trust in Jesus.

PRAYER

Heavenly Father, I believe in what Jesus did for me on the cross. My sins were laid on His body. My shame was transferred to His account. He took my place so I can take His. I am in Christ, seated at the Father's right hand. I am righteous, justified, forgiven and completely free from the bondage of sin.

Chapter 9:
We are acceptable to God

For the law having a shadow of good things to come, and not the very image of the things, can never with those sacrifices which they offered year by year continually make the comers thereunto perfect. For then would they not have ceased to be offered? because that the worshippers once purged should have had no more conscience of sins. But in those sacrifices there is a remembrance again made of sins every year.
Hebrews 10:1–3 (KJV)

A few years ago, just after I had passed my driving test, I was feeling pleased that I had accomplished this milestone. I drove to church and into the car park (parking lot), where I struggled with reversing into a space between two parked cars. I tried going in forward, but did not want to risk hitting the parked cars. Then I tried reversing into the space but just couldn't. It was a huge struggle.

While I was still figuring out what to do next, another man drove into the car park, and in no time easily parked his car in an empty space, got out and walked away. 'Wow! What a show off!' I thought to myself. 'Just a few more practices and a little more confidence, I'll do better than this.' My lovely wife who sat next to me looked at me and said, 'Did you see that?' I responded 'so what? Do you want to seat in his car so you can get reversed into the parking lot quicker?' We ended the discussion right there!

I continued to negotiate many little turns, repeatedly trying to park the car. I did it over and over again to get it right. It took several attempts before I finally made it. Eventually, after another fifteen minutes, I managed to park the car. Compared to the other man, who may have had years of experience, I was a fledgling at driving and had to continuously repeat the same actions until I got it right.

This reminds me of one of the many roles of the Old Testament high priests. They offered a sacrifice every year for the remission of sins for the nation of Israel. The offerings never brought about perfection of the nation's conscience. In fact, the opposite was true. It brought a consciousness of sin to the people offering the sacrifices. The people always had a debt of sin on their conscience. The sacrifices only brought about a temporary covering of sins and a constant reminder that they were all sinners. However, our Lord Jesus, who is our Great High Priest (greater than all other high priests), offered a perfect sacrifice once and for all. His offering was so perfect the very first time He offered Himself that there was no further need to repeat the sacrifice. Unlike the Old Testament priests, who offered animal sacrifices yearly, our Lord Jesus offered His own blood once which avails forever. After He offered Himself as the sacrifice, He sat down, denoting a completion of a perfectly finished work with nothing left to do.

Today our Great High Priest has not covered our sins, He has removed them. He has taken them away. We are not temporarily forgiven; we are permanently and completely forgiven. We are perfected forever by one sacrifice, and now have a perfect conscience. There is no more offering of sins because our Lord Jesus took away all our sins and paid completely for them on the cross of Calvary. What a perfect work our Saviour did on the cross. Today, His shed blood makes us completely perfect and acceptable to God.

PRAYER
Thank You, Lord, that I am seated with Christ Jesus in the heavenly places, far above principalities and powers. I am perfected forever by the one sacrifice of Jesus Christ. I no longer have a conscience with sin debt. Your perfect sacrifice makes my conscience perfect.

Chapter 10:

God helps those who believe him

I will lift up mine eyes unto the hills, from whence cometh my help. My help cometh from the LORD, which made heaven and earth.

Psalm 121:1–2 (KJV)

We all have heard the saying 'God helps those who help themselves'. Only recently, I discovered that this was a phrase used by Benjamin Franklin when he quoted Aesop's Fables. God helps those who put their trust in Him (see Psalm 20).

When the children of Israel came out of the land of bondage, they left Egypt for the Promised Land. Their exit from Egypt was a direct result of God's help. God sent ten plagues to Pharaoh, the last of which caused him to let the people go (see Exodus, chapters 7–11).

Not even a week out of Egypt, at the brink of the Red Sea, they needed help with the crossing. They started complaining to Moses, their leader, but God's grace was sufficient, and through

Moses' rod, God parted the Red Sea so that they crossed over on dry ground and were not captured by the Egyptians (Exodus 14).

In Exodus 15, only three days after crossing the Red Sea, they found no water. They were quick to forget who had helped them previously, and started murmuring and complaining to Moses. Again God helped them, healing the bitter waters of Marah. God did not object to their complaints but went ahead, revealing Himself for the first time in Scripture as their healer: 'If you listen carefully to the Lord your God and do what is right in his eyes, if you pay attention to his commands and keep all his decrees, I will not bring on you any of the diseases I brought on the Egyptians, for I am the Lord, who heals you' (Exodus 15:26).

About a month after leaving Egypt, they murmured again. As soon as they were hungry and ran out of supplies, God's grace was seen again as He rained bread from heaven. Again and again, they had no means to help themselves and complained to Moses, who in turn talked to God about the people's need. God's grace was seen every step of the way. It was revealed in crossing the Red Sea, in providing for their need, in quenching their thirst, in healing the bitter waters of Marah and in satisfying their hunger.

If only had they fully recognised the grace of God – that inexhaustible, never-ending supply and never-failing grace – they would have remained under it. They would not have made the unanimous prideful decision to keep all of God's commands without His help.

Everything took a different turn when they came to the foot of the mountain. They denied their need for God's help and thought their own ability and strength could carry them through. Their confidence was now shifted from God to themselves. When Moses relayed God's instructions to the people, they boasted in their own strength and proudly took succour in their ability to keep all of God's commandments. Not counting the cost, their response was filled with pride. They were highly opinionated in their strength to keep God's Law. Not counting the cost or realising what was involved, they cried with one glib, unanimous voice, 'All the Lord has spoken will we do' (Exodus 19:8). So they put themselves under Law.[2] The moment they collectively responded to Moses, God changed His method of dealing with them. The Law was given and the Ten Commandments were given to the children of Israel. Within two weeks, the same people who boasted in their ability to keep all of God's Law had already broken the first and were found guilty as they danced lewdly worshipping the golden calf.

God does not want you to depend on self-help or confidence in the flesh. Instead He wants you to depend on His grace. The prophet Jeremiah makes a comparison between those who put their trust in themselves and those who put their trust in God. He says the one who trusts in himself is already empowered to

---

[2] Meyers, F B (1951), *The way into the Holiest*, Grand Rapids Michigan: Baker Book House.

fail. That person is so infatuated with himself that they don't see opportunity when it comes.

This is what the Lord says: 'Cursed is the one who trusts in man, who draws strength from mere flesh and whose heart turns away from the Lord. That person will be like a bush in the wastelands; they will not see prosperity when it comes. They will dwell in the parched places of the desert, in a salt land where no one lives.'

Jeremiah 17:5–6

However, the one who trusts and puts their confidence in God is empowered to succeed, regardless of what season of life they find themselves in.

But blessed is the one who trusts in the Lord, whose confidence is in him. They will be like a tree planted by the water that sends out its roots by the stream. It does not fear when heat comes; its leaves are always green. It has no worries in a year of drought and never fails to bear fruit.

Jeremiah 17:7–8

God does not help people who help themselves, instead His sufficient help is lavishly unleashed in the lives of those who admit they cannot help themselves and put their trust and confidence in Him. Today, God wants you to trust His grace. It is the grace of God that empowers us and allows us to meet every demand in life so we can do all God has called us to accomplish.

PRAYER

My trust is in the Lord. I do not rely on my ability, strength, wisdom or accomplishments. I trust in You, Lord. Today, I can't, but You can, therefore let Your grace flow into every area of my life. Thank you for pouring out Your grace on me so I can face life today, winning in every situation.

Chapter 11:
All Things Are Working Together For Our Good

And we know that in all things God works for the good of those who love him, who have been called according to his purpose.

Romans 8:28

God can cause all things, both good and bad, to work in our favour. There are seasons in life when it seems you are in a drought and times when you question God's presence. There are days when we don't sense His closeness or His presence in our lives. My friend, these are the times you should be even more conscious of His ever-abiding presence in your life. He is closer to you than the breath in your nostrils. When we go through trying seasons in life, be reassured that God is not the author of evil. He is not the author of sickness or disease. He is not the one who caused us to lose our jobs or something dear to us. He only bestows good gifts to His children.

> *Every good and perfect gift is from above, coming down from the Father of the heavenly lights, who does not change like shifting shadows.*
>
> **James 1:17**

Jesus reveals His very heart to His disciples as the giver of life, both in quality and quantity. He also reveals in the Gospel of John who the devil is and what he aims to achieve.

> *The thief comes only to steal and kill and destroy; I have come that they may have life, and have it to the full.*
>
> **John 10:10**

Joseph, who was sold into slavery, understood the part God played in his times of trial. Here is a man who was hated by his brothers and thrown into a well, then sold to Potiphar and falsely accused by Potiphar's wife. As a result, he was thrown into prison. Joseph knew that God did not cause his predicament. God did not cause Joseph's brothers to hate him nor Potiphar's wife to lie about him, but they did. Yet in the midst of Joseph's predicament, God's favour was on him. From the pit to the prison to the palace, Joseph was surrounded by the favour of God. The Lord was with him.

With the favour of God, God can cause all evil plans to turn out good for His children. He can turn the worst scenario into the best scenario. He can take a stumbling block and transform it into a stepping stone, and makes things designed against us work for us. All things work together for our highest good.

My wife and I drove down a familiar lane one Saturday morning. It was raining lightly and visibility was OK. Before we left home, our son had asked if he could come with us, but we had insisted he stayed at home with his sister. As we drove down a hill, I lost control of the car. It was as if the car's steering was not working any longer. The car skidded out of control, did a complete 360-degree turn and crashed into a fence. The impact pushed the boot (trunk) of the car inwards and the car was written off by the insurance company.

The Lord preserved us all and we came out of the accident unhurt, without a scratch. A few months before, we had been contemplating getting a loan for another car as the one we drove had seen better days. In fact, because of the high mileage on the car, it was almost worthless. God certainly was not the author of the car accident, yet He used it as a means of providing supernaturally for us. The insurance company wrote the car off and the underwriters gave us a cheque for almost five times its value. Now that's God's grace! Not only were we preserved but God provided as well. A few weeks before the accident, I had the privilege of listening to a message titled 'The promise of Protection –Truths from Psalm 91'. In this message, Pastor Prince talked about locating the secret place. He said the secret place is being justified by faith, staying in faith and not returning to the law. I was encouraged not to even trust my many years of driving experience but the Lord who is our refuge and hiding place.

God can take the worst strategy that Satan comes up with and turn it for our highest good. God took the worst instrument of cruelty invented by man – crucifixion – and turned it into a gracious means by which people can be saved. As a result of Adam's disobedience, death came into the world. Yet for the believer, God uses death as a means by which we are promoted to glory.

Whatever life throws at you, you are fully equipped to come out on top. All things are working together for your good. If life throws eggs at us, we see it as an ingredient for an omelette. If life throws lemons at us, instead of sucking on sour lemon, we see it as an ingredient for lemonade.

> *As they pass through the Valley of Baka, they make it a place of springs; the autumn rains also cover it with pools.*
> **Psalm 84:6**

When we go through the valley of weeping, we turn it into a place of spring.

Joseph concluded in the later part of his life, referring to his brothers: 'You intended to harm me, but God intended it for good to accomplish what is now being done, the saving of many lives' (Genesis 50:20).

PRAYER

Thank You, Father, because all things are working for my good right now. You always cause us to triumph in every situation through Christ Jesus. I am winning in all circumstances because You are with me.

Chapter 12:
Shouts of 'Grace, Grace'

Then he answered and spake unto me, saying, This is the word of the Lord unto Zerubbabel, saying, Not by might, nor by power, but by my spirit, saith the Lord of hosts. Who art thou, O great mountain? before Zerubbabel thou shalt become a plain: and he shall bring forth the headstone thereof with shoutings, crying, Grace, grace unto it.

Zechariah 4:6–7 (KJV)

Leaders lead and followers follow: where the leader goes, followers gravitate. The Bible compares a leader and their followers to the relationship between a shepherd and their sheep. The sheep will follow the leading of the good shepherd. Leaders are under shepherds of God's people, and as leaders God has entrusted us with the responsibility of feeding and caring for the flock.

Every organisation thrives on leadership. Leaders with direction, vision and clarity of purpose have the ability to share their hearts with those around them and forge a way towards accomplishing the set goals. If the leaders are excited about God and the plans

He has for them, the followers will easily be inspired to get to know God's plan for their lives too. But if the leader lacks purpose, excitement and clarity, the same traits will be reflected in the lives of the followers.

Most of us are leaders to some degree or another. You may be leading your family as a husband or a parent. You may be a top executive of a Fortune 500 company or a student in the first year studying for a degree. Whatever we do, we are leading our lives to some extent. As we walk through life, satan has a way of throwing curve balls at us. The devil sometimes uses situations and people to hinder what God is doing in and through us.

Two great leaders in the Bible experienced great resistance and opposition to the assignment God gave them. Joshua the high priest and Zerubbabel the governor, together with the people of Judah, had just returned from exile to rebuild the ruins of God's temple. It all started OK, but then their enemies opposed them. The Samaritans wrote a letter to the king, making accusations against the children of Israel. In this letter they urged the king to bring the work to a stop. Eventually the king gave in and sent a decree to stop the building of the temple. The accusations brought against the children of Israel put a halt to the progress of the building project.

Are you in that place today? Are there things in your life about which you once were excited but which now seem to be on hold? Perhaps you started writing a book, but halfway through you gave up. Maybe it is a failed relationship that now hinders you from trying again. Perhaps you failed an examination twice and have now given up on education. You may have concluded, 'What's the point trying again? I just haven't got what it takes.'

Whatever it is, the great news is that you *can* get back up again and start building, no matter how long your vision or dreams have been put on hold.

For fifteen years, Joshua, Zechariah and the children of Israel pulled back from building God's temple because of this one reason: accusation. As the leaders went, so too did the people. The people went home and started building their own houses and left the house of God in ruins.

You see, long before there is a stop to the dream or the vision, long before you give up on your desires, Satan brings accusation to your mind. Usually he does this by reminding you of your past mistakes and regrets, suggesting to you that these disqualify you from going ahead with your plans. He says things like 'Your past relationship failed because you were just not there, and so this too will fail because relationships are not designed for people like you.' He reminds you of your childhood regrets and says things like 'You never had the privilege of going to a good school – how can you ever make it in life?'

Friends, we all have past regrets and mistakes, but God does not want you to be regretful for the past and lose out on the great blessings He has for you today. We learn from our mistakes and look to Jesus to help us now. Don't receive the devil's accusation. You are not your past; you are a new creation in Christ Jesus.

So God raised two prophets to speak to these leaders who were depressed. The message God gave the leaders through the prophets had to do with how they saw themselves, and with the grace of God. To Joshua the high priest, God gave Zechariah a message that his filthy garment had been changed. So God's message to Joshua was about how he saw himself. Joshua saw himself as filthy. Perhaps it was something he had done in the past that caused him to see himself that way. Whatever it was, God had a better plan and instead clothed him with a garment of righteousness (Zechariah 3:1–4). To Zerubbabel, the message was that the temple would not be built by strength or his ability, but by the spirit of the Lord. God also told him that the capstone (the final phase) of the building would be set in place as he shouted 'Grace, grace' (Zechariah 4:7 KJV).

One leader needed to see himself as the righteousness of God in Christ, and the other needed more revelation on the grace of God.[3] As soon as the Word of God was delivered to these leaders, they were back in favour with the king and they started building. A project that had been left in ruins for fifteen years was accomplished in only four years.

---

[3] Joseph Prince, *Actively possess your forgiveness in Christ* (CD Sermon), 19 October 2014. Singapore: Joseph Prince Resources.

Friends, once you refuse to receive the devil's accusation and are conscious of what Jesus has done for you on the cross of Calvary, then the grace of God can flow. You are not the mistake of your past; you are a new creation in Christ Jesus. Your dreams and desires will not be accomplished by your natural strength or the lack of it, but by God's grace. Get back and start building from where you left off. You will finish well, with shouts of 'Grace, grace'!

PRAYER

I am not condemned. I do not accept Satan's accusation. There is therefore no condemnation to me, because I am in Christ Jesus. I am the righteousness of God in Christ. I am saved by grace. Today, whatever I touch will prosper and all I do will be successful. I'm a finisher and I will finish well. Thank You Jesus.

Chapter 13:
Complete in Him, lacking nothing

He said, "If you listen carefully to the LORD your God and do what is right in his eyes, if you pay attention to his commands and keep all his decrees, I will not bring on you any of the diseases I brought on the Egyptians, for I am the LORD, who heals you."

Exodus 15:26

Are you believing God for the healing of your physical body or that of a loved one? Well, I'd like to share a testimony from a member of our church who God healed completely from an ear infection. I hope this will encourage you. God still heals today and can do the same for you and your loved ones.

The devil tried to rob me of my hearing. I went to bed one night and woke up the next morning not able to hear in my right ear. In fact, when spoken to, I hardly heard anyone until I was nudged or jostled to get my attention. This persisted for a few days, and it then developed into a migraine and I experienced lots of pain on the side of my neck very close to my right ear. This continued for almost a month. I dreaded the thought of having to get a hearing aid at a very young age in life. The thought of losing my hearing and not being able to hear my son was very disturbing.

I went to the doctor's, but the doctor, having done a thorough examination of the ear, said there was nothing in there. They found nothing wrong! One Sunday, I came to church and sat under the Word. I told God, 'Father, I am Your child, so please take care of this.' As the Word was being preached, I felt something move in my ear. No sooner than putting my finger into my ear, I had to make a move for the restroom because of what came out of my ears! In the restroom, the more I cleaned my ears, the more wax came out. That Sunday, I regained 50 per cent of my hearing. The following day, there was no more pain. The migraine disappeared. That week, I thanked God for healing me while in church. But I was not content with a 50 per cent healing. I wanted complete healing so I could hear fully. Nothing much happened that week. There were no emissions: nothing at all. I came back to church the following Sunday. The Word was being preached and again exactly the same thing happened to the ears. Again, I had to stand up to excuse myself. After cleaning up my ears, this time I was completely healed and received full recovery of my hearing. Praise God!

During each meeting, the gospel of grace was being preached. The crux of the message was that Jesus died on the cross to make us righteous. There is nothing we can do to earn righteousness. It has to be received as a gift. On the cross, Jesus paid for our sins and also the healing of our body. The same body that bore our sins, carried our sickness. 'By his stripes we are healed' (Isaiah 53:5).

Friend, you may be releasing your faith for healing and restoration. Or you may be releasing your faith for the healing of a loved one. Here is something profound you need to know. You don't have to be in a church service for God to heal your body. He can heal you right where you are even right now. Jesus on the cross of Calvary paid for the forgiveness of your sins. Once you receive Him, you are completely forgiven of all your sins. He also paid for all of our sickness and took it all upon Himself. Today, because of Jesus you are the righteousness of God in Christ. As the righteousness of God in Christ, sickness cannot coexist in your body. The doctors may have given a diagnosis that seems contradictory to what you are believing for but don't be dismayed. Jesus Christ of Nazareth is your healer and even right now He is healing you and making you whole.

Prayer
Father, thank you that by faith I am the righteousness of God in Christ. Jesus bore my sins on the cross. He carried all my grief and pains. He took my place on the cross that I may take His place. I am healed, whole, sound, complete and well.

CHAPTER 14:

THE SUBSTANCE OF MY AFFECTION

They asked each other, "Were not our hearts burning within us while he talked with us on the road and opened the Scriptures to us?"

Luke 24:32

After Jesus was crucified on the cross, His disciples were so sad and despondent at His death. They were saddened by the fact that the Jews had crucified their Messiah, and they had forgotten what Jesus said concerning His death.

As they walked on the way to Emmaus, Jesus drew close to them, talked with them but He withheld their eyes from seeing Him! They did not even know it was Jesus who talked with them. The disciples were tired and depleted – almost at their wits' end. However, Jesus kept on talking to them. He discussed the scriptures from the book of Moses to the Prophets. He talked to them about Himself. Knowing full well how the disciples felt, Jesus addressed the root cause of their anxiety and calmed every fear by going through the scriptures, revealing Himself to them.

Many accounts of Jesus' conversations in the Bible show that He talked about Himself. For example, in Matthew 16: 'After He was finally rejected by his own, He turned to His disciples and asked them "Who do men say that I Am?"' The conversation was about Him. Then in the following chapter, on the Mount of Transfiguration, again the conversation between Jesus and his disciples focused on how He was going to conquer death on the cross and rise again. It was always about Him.

As He expounded the scriptures to the despondent disciples on the Emmaus Road, perhaps He revealed Himself as the Tree of Life in the Garden of Eden and the animal God killed to clothe Adam and Eve. He must have discussed the five Levitical offerings: the sin offering, burnt offering, trespass offering, meal offering and peace offering. He must have shown them that He was the Passover Lamb whose blood was put on the lintels and door posts of the Israelites when they were about to leave Egypt. As He spoke to them they must have seen Him in the scriptures as the tabernacle in the wilderness and the sacrificial animal offered to God. He must have said He was the Rock that travelled with them in the wilderness and was the bronze serpent on the pole upon whom all our sins were judged and whoever believed in Him was saved. Oh, what a beautiful exposition that must have been!

Finally, they got to their destination and sat for supper. Jesus was going to leave them and they compelled Him to stay for dinner. No sooner had they eaten the bread that Jesus had broken and given to them than their eyes were opened. The moment they knew Jesus, He disappeared from their midst. Something happened after they partook of the bread. When Adam and Eve ate from the tree of knowledge of good and evil, they knew they were naked and became self-conscious; when the disciples ate of the bread of life, they became conscious not of themselves but of Him. They found a new passion and a zest for life. A new wind came about. They were reinvigorated with strength. They said, one to another, 'Did our hearts not burn when He talked to us?' They were set ablaze. Their hearts were set on fire. They got up and that same night walked back to Jerusalem strong!

Have you ever been so despondent and carried away by the magnitude of a problem that even when the answer shows up you don't see it, because you are so consumed and almost strangled by the tentacles of the problem?

1 Corinthians 10:13 says 'No temptation has overtaken you except what is common to mankind. And God is faithful; he will not let you be tempted beyond what you can bear. But when you are tempted, he will also provide a way out so that you can endure it.'

Are you in the place of trials where you are so overwhelmed by the enormity of your problem that you don't even see the way out that God has provided?

Do you feel tired? Or worn out? Have you been believing and standing on the promises of God for so long that you are beginning to wonder whether it will come to pass or not? There is something about looking to Jesus that gives us a new lease of life and strength. When we feed on Him and see Him for who He is through His Word, we are renewed in our strength. As Isaiah said, 'they that wait on the Lord shall renew their strength'. As the despondent disciples waited on the Lord by receiving His gracious words, their strength was renewed.

PRAYER

Jesus, I look to You. You are everything to me. My strength is in You. My hope and trust is in You. My heart burns afresh today with a passion for life. I can do all things through Christ who strengthens me. I shake off everything that acts as a distraction and keep my eyes on You. You are the centre of my life and the substance of my affection.

Chapter 15:
The Sufficiency of Grace

Three times I pleaded with the Lord to take it away from me. But he said to me "My grace is sufficient for you, for my power is made perfect in weakness." Therefore I will boast all the more gladly about my weaknesses, so that Christ's power may rest on me. That is why, for Christ's sake, I delight in weaknesses, in insults, in hardships, in persecutions, in difficulties. For when I am weak, then I am strong.
2 Corinthians 12:8–10 (NIV)

When you see lack, what do you think? When you see weakness, what do you think? When you feel unable to accomplish a task at hand, how do you react or what do you do?

Many people who feel insufficient in and of themselves only resolve to stay that way. They feel they don't know much, don't have much and therefore can't help much because of their limited resources. You may have heard teaching about focusing on your strengths and not on your weakness. The world says our weaknesses are disadvantages, but Jesus says He can work with your weakness and that's the very thing He wants.

Paul shows us how, through the grace of God, we can be empowered during times of weaknesses. He says 'When I am weak, then I am strong. When I am poor, then I am rich. In my weakness, the power of God can flow through me.'

To Paul, lack and not having enough were no indication that he would never have or be without. Lack only created an opportunity for Paul to see the power of God magnified in that area of his life. Being weak does not mean you will remain without strength. It is just an opportunity for you to see the strength of God manifested in the very area of your insufficiencies.

The little boy's five loaves of bread and two pieces of fish were wholly inadequate to meet the voracious appetite of the hungry multitude in Luke 9:13. Yet this little boy's dinner was what the Lord chose to magnify His grace and goodness so much so that the crowd was well fed and there were twelve baskets left over.

The widowed wife of a prophet also witnessed the superabundant supply of God's provision in the very area of her lack (2 Kings 4:1–7). She went from a place of being indebted to her creditors to a place where she had more than enough to live on with her children. God's supply was magnified in the very area of lack.

Lazarus experienced the resurrection power of God as he was raised from the dead (John 11).

Lack, insufficiencies, inadequacies – for the believer these are only pointers to the superfluous empowering, superabundant, never-ending supply of God s grace.

The very area in which you feel insufficient is the very area God wants to glorify Himself. So instead of running away from God because of your weakness, run to Him so His glory may be magnified in your life. Completely depend on His grace with the little you have and see what masterpiece the grace of God can make out of you.

I wrote this book not because I am a fountain of knowledge in the teaching of God's grace. Not because I know a lot; in fact, I don't know much. However, the one thing I do know is that even in the area of my limited knowledge and resources, God's grace is magnified in those areas. The less of self I assert, the more of Him I experience. Don't let your limitations stop you from experiencing God's best for you. It is not about you, it is all about Him. So I hope the little I know and have written with God's abundance of grace makes a marked difference in your life.

PRAYER
Thank You, Father, for Your grace. Jesus is my sufficiency. With Him I am complete and lack nothing. Transform my life with Your grace and make it count in my generation for Your glory.

Chapter 16:

His Finished Work Is Our Resting Ground

When he had received the drink, Jesus said, "It is finished." With that, he bowed his head and gave up his spirit.

John 19:30

It is one thing to finish a race but another to finish in style. What's more important than completing a task is the finishing detail with which the task is completed. God loves to finish in style. When He created the heavens and earth, He rested on the seventh day. He rested not because He was tired but because He had finished and there was nothing left to do.

The first words of Jesus in the New Testament were 'Don't you know I'm about my Father's business' and His last word was 'Finished'. He said 'finished' on the cross not because the soldiers took His life from Him, but because there was nothing left to do. No one could take His life from Him; He willingly offered it for the sins of the world. On the cross, our sins, which were condemned on His body once and for all, were put away. There, He nailed the Law and ordinances to the cross and completely paid the penalty of our all sins.

Today, God is not counting your sins against you, because it was finished on the cross. If Jesus cried out 'it is finished', then it is finished. God cannot be angry with you because He exhausted his anger on the body of a substitute. Just as God rested when He was finished with creation, and Jesus rested His head after He cried out 'finished', we can rest in the finished work of Jesus. We begin from where He finished. Our starting posture is one of resting in Jesus' finished work.

We rest knowing that everything needed has already been done. There is nothing we can do to better the perfect work of Jesus on the cross. Our attempts to make better or improve on what Jesus did, through our effort and works, are futile and only bring to nought God's promises in our lives. Any attempt to add to what Jesus did on the cross of Calvary is the greatest insult one can give to God, who gave His only Son for us. The finished work of Jesus on the cross is perfect, complete and cannot get any better by the best of human noble exertions or even righteous deeds.

Today Jesus is seated at the right hand of the Father, not because He is God's Son, for He always has been, but because He put away our sins once and for all and gave His life as a perfect sacrifice for us. (Hebrews 1:3 says: 'The Son is the radiance of God's glory and the exact representation of his being, sustaining all things by his powerful word. After he had provided purification for sins, he sat down at the right hand of the Majesty in heaven.') The greatest pleasure we can bring to God is rest in the finished work of Jesus. His finished work is our resting ground.

As you begin your day, begin with the consciousness that Jesus did it all, and everything you need for life and godliness is already provided.

PRAYER

Thank You, Lord Jesus, for Your finished work on the cross of Calvary. I rest in what You did for me. Your finished work is my resting ground. I am not worried, and I am not stressed. I rest in Your work and so I'm blessed.

CHAPTER 17:
THE UPLIFTING POWER OF GRACE

But Jesus took him by the hand and lifted him to his feet, and he stood up.

Mark 9:27

Have you ever tried suppressing an inflated balloon under water? It only stays there as long as you hold it down. But as soon as you let go, it always pops back and stays afloat. That's who you are in Christ. You are like an inflated balloon that always rises to the top, regardless of any setback life throws at you.

What keeps the balloon afloat is its content, air. Because air is lighter than water, it will always float on water. If the same balloon is filled with sand or gravel, it will sink when pushed beneath water. What keeps you going is Who is in you. Life has its own way of pulling you down. Satan brings situations into our lives not to lift us up but to pull us down. Eventually he has a mission to destroy the individual. His job description is to steal, kill and destroy (John 10:10). He gains access into people's lives through the door of guilt or condemnation or maybe even with just a suggestive thought that they are not good enough. If we believe and accept these negative thoughts into our lives, we will get weighed down. Fear then creeps in, and like Adam and Eve, we will feel as if we no longer measure up to what God says about us. Instead, refuse to accept the devil's accusation and condemnation and like an inflated balloon, you will stand tall in every area of your life. Just like the balloon gets weighed down by the sand, Satan tries to weigh us down with his condemnation.

Jesus said my yoke is easy and my burden is light. Jesus is the air that keeps the balloon floating. With Him in your heart, no matter what life throws at you, you always stay afloat because He has won the ultimate victory for us.

Matthew 17 tells us about what happened on the Mount of Transfiguration, when only Peter, James and John were with Jesus. A voice came from heaven, saying 'Listen to him!' The disciples were afraid and fell down. Instead of Jesus rebuking the disciples, He touched them and said 'Get up, don't be afraid'. In the same chapter, a father brings his demon-possessed son to Jesus' disciples for healing. They were not able to cast out the devil and so he made his way to Jesus. After Jesus rebuked the dumb and deaf spirit in the boy, he was healed immediately. The Gospel of Mark gives us an insight to what happens afterwards.

> *But Jesus took him by the hand and lifted him to his feet, and he stood up.*
>
> **Mark 9:27**

In both accounts, Jesus demonstrated the uplifting power of grace.

On one hand, the disciples were afraid of the light and fell. On the other hand, a demon possessed a little boy, and after it was cast out the little boy fell. Jesus lifts them both. Today, allow yourself to be lifted by Jesus. No matter what life has thrown at you, refuse to remain in the posture of self-pity and condemnation. Lift your eyes up today and be lifted by Jesus. Let His grace fill your life so you can stand on your feet winning, conquering and always victorious.

PRAYER
Today I allow myself to be lifted by Your mighty and strong hands. My confidence is not in my grip on You but in the unbreakable grip of Your mighty hands on my life. I can sail through the storm and when others say there is a casting down, I declare there is a lifting up. I arise from every depth of condemnation and guilt. I allow Your life and grace to fill me up so I can soar high in life.

Chapter 18:

Redeemed from sickness

Dear friend, I pray that you may enjoy good health and that all may go well with you, even as your soul is getting along well.

3 John 1:2

Do you feel sick in your body? Or have you just received a diagnosis from the doctor about a condition you have always dreaded? Are you moved by the failing health of a loved one? God loves you so much and He wants it well with you and your loved ones.

A few years back, after finishing my studies and a long search for the right position, I secured a job as a medical sales rep for a prestigious company. I was so excited about this opportunity and wanted to share my experience with my then fiancée, Bakang. I looked forward to narrating the whole interview experience with her over dinner and booked an idyllic restaurant that overlooked the River Thames in London Town.

Bakang had travelled down for a church conference, and during an intermission between sessions we went for dinner. I had rehearsed my presentation many times over. I just knew she would be proud of this good-looking man. She was already impressed with me because she had said yes to my marriage proposal. I still wanted to impress her some more. We walked into the restaurant with soft music playing. The lights were set just right, it was the perfect ambience in which to enjoy each other's company.

I placed the order with the waiter, and while the meal was being prepared, we were treated to a bowl filled with a mixture of spicy and tasty nuts. Without hesitating, I dipped my fingers into the bowl on the table between me and Bakang and threw a handful into my mouth. Something weird happened almost immediately. As I was just about to tell her about the interview day experience, I was interrupted with an itch. I found my hands reaching down to scratch, but just thought 'Behave, Bayo, you are eating! This is the dinner table!' So I tried to keep cool and ignore it. This was just impossibly unbearable. So I stood up to give my buttock a good scratch. Bakang looked at me with a bewildered look on her face and said, 'Are you ok?' I responded with a brash 'yes' and carried on scratching, by which time my body was under attack. I excused myself, rushed to the bathroom and looked my face in the mirror. It was covered with hives. So was my body. I was having an allergic reaction to the nuts! I was rushed to the hospital and was treated that night for a nut allergy and later discharged. I did not manage to finish dinner and of course the account of the interview experience waited for another day.

A few months later, whilst studying the Word of God, I realised that itching was part of the curse.

> *The Lord will afflict you with the boils of Egypt and with tumors, festering sores and the itch, from which you cannot be cured.*
>
> **Deuteronomy 28:27**

I realised that when Jesus died on the cross, He paid for all my sins and redeemed me from the curse of the Law, including itching. My faith for healing was so stirred up that one day I felt like nibbling on something after a long day's work. There was nothing to nibble on except some nuts! I ate them without thinking twice. For some reason I had forgotten about the allergic reaction experience. A few days later I remembered I had eaten nuts, but did not react to them. Wow! Indeed I am redeemed from the curse of the Law. (Please note that this is my personal experience and not a recommendation for you to do.)

I have heard people draw conclusions from the above scripture in Deuteronomy that sickness is from God and sometimes uses it as a teaching material for His children. Now God is not the author of sickness or disease. He never employs sicknes to teach His children lessons on healing. He is not insecure and will never prove He is a healer by making His children sick and later heal them.

Dr Robert Young, the author of *A Commentary on The Holy Bible*, points out that in the Hebrew language in which the Old Testament was written, the verb used to describe God is permissive rather than causative. The verb means God permitted the disease and affliction of the children of Israel but did not cause it. Commenting on a similar verse – Exodus 10:1 – Robert Young explains how God permitted Pharaoh's heart to be hardened. He comments: 'the causative (or Hiphil) form of the Hebrew verb is often simply permissive or declarative, as have been already noticed, and as is universally admitted by all Biblical critics.'[4]

So, Deuteronomy 28:27 should read 'The Lord will permit or allow the curse' instead of saying it is God that caused the curse.

The curse came on the children of Israel when they did not obey God's commands. As a result, they took themselves away from God's protection and were susceptible to Satan's weapons.

Today, God is not treating you based on your ability to keep the Law and obey the commandments. As a believer, He is treating you based on the perfect work Jesus accomplished on the cross of Calvary. On the cross, all our sickness and disease were laid on Him. He carried all our pain and sorrow so that we can walk in healing and divine health. By the stripes of Jesus on the cross,

---

[4] Robert Young, (1868), *A commentary on the Holy Bible*, New York: A. Fullerton & Co.

you are healed. You are redeemed from every type of infection and malady. Jesus Christ of Nazareth is your healer, so be made whole today in Jesus' name.

PRAYER

I receive my healing now. Jesus Christ of Nazareth is my healer. I confess that by Your stripes on the cross of Calvary, I am healed.

Chapter 19:
God is a Happy God

"To me this is like the days of Noah, when I swore that the waters of Noah would never again cover the earth. So now I have sworn not to be angry with you, never to rebuke you again. Though the mountains be shaken and the hills be removed, yet my unfailing love for you will not be shaken nor my covenant of peace be removed," says the Lord, who has compassion on you.

Isaiah 54:9–10

You have probably heard the saying 'perception is everything'. This is a profound statement because how you see God will set your expectation of Him.

How do you view God today? Do you see Him as a furious king waiting for His subjects to fail, only to use His mighty power against them? Do you view Him as the author of sickness and disease? The one who kills and takes away precious lives, including those of little children? Isn't it interesting to watch the news and see how major catastrophic world occurrences such as a volcanic eruption, an earthquake, a plane crash or a wildfire are always described as 'acts of God'?

It is very sad to see how God is portrayed as an angry king, executing judgement on His children in order to keep them in check. There is nothing farther from the truth than this outrageous depiction of our God. Yes, it is true that God is holy and just. He is a righteous judge over all the earth (Psalm 11:7). As He is righteous, every wrong has to be punished, the penalty for sin has to be paid, and the sentence for an offence has to be served. If sin were to go unpunished, it would undermine the nature of a holy God and impinge upon the character of a just God.

What happens when a righteous God comes into contact with a sinful human? Punishment resulting in divine wrath. The first case of this is found in the Garden of Eden. God gave Adam and Eve a garden with everything they needed and asked them to freely eat of every tree with the exception of one: the tree of knowledge of good and evil. He also told them what would happen should they eat from the tree.

> *The Lord God took the man and put him in the Garden of Eden to work it and take care of it. And the Lord God commanded the man, "You are free to eat from any tree in the garden; but you must not eat from the tree of the knowledge of good and evil, for when you eat from it you will certainly die."*
>
> **Genesis 2:15–17**

These first people, who were created with a free will, decided to go against God's instruction and ate from the tree: the first case of sin recorded in the Bible. As a holy God, sin has to be punished. God's divine wrath against the sin of man was executed, but on the body of a substitute. In Genesis 3:21, The Lord God made garments of skin for Adam and Eve and clothed them. That day, an animal died, blood was shed, a garment was made and Adam and Eve were clothed. God punished the sin of Adam and Eve using the body of a temporary substitute – the sacrificial animal – and then completely took it away in the body of Jesus on the cross. There in the garden, the justice of God, displayed in His divine wrath to punish sin by death, was merged with the love of God demonstrated in executing the punishment of sin in the body of a substitute. God hates sin but loves the sinner. God's righteousness and love are united in the killing of an animal. The degree to which God loves the sinner is the same degree to which He hates sin.

This righteous act displayed in the Garden of Eden would later be amplified in the body of Jesus on the cross. The righteousness and mercy of God 'kiss' at the cross. Jesus was the lamb that was slain from the foundation of the world (Revelation 13:8). On the cross of Calvary, the body of Jesus as a payment for the sins of the whole world upheld the justice and righteousness of God and magnified the love of God. The body of Jesus was a public display of the love of the Father for the world to see. Jesus was made a sin offering for us on the cross. He who knew no sin became sin for us (2 Corinthians 5:21). All of our wrongdoing from the Garden of Eden, all of our sins and unrighteous acts were transferred to the account of Jesus. Every sin we ever committed from the day we were born to the day we stand before Him was all calculated and laid on the body of Jesus as He hung on the cross. On the cross, the holiness of God met with the sinfulness of man on the body of Jesus. God's righteous anger and indignation were exhausted and completely drained on the body of Jesus and whosoever believes in the sacrifice of Jesus is given a free pardon.

Today, God is not angry with you, because all his anger burnt furiously for a moment on the body of Jesus. Jesus was made sin for us, so that we can be made the righteousness of God. Just as our sin was credited to His account on the cross, His righteousness is credited to the account of those who believe and are justly forgiven. You are clothed with the coat of God's righteousness and God is pleased with you because of Jesus. The God of the Bible; our God is a happy God. He's got a big smile on His face and wants to do you so much good all because of Jesus. He wants to heal your broken heart; He wants to provide for you and yours. He wants to heal your child and grant you favour with people. This is the God we serve. He loves you so much.

PRAYER

Thank You, Jesus, for displaying Your love for me on the cross. God was pleased with Your sacrifice and raised You for my justification. Today I have right standing with God and expect God's grace to shine on me. I have access to God's favour knowing you are not against me but for me. Thank You Jesus.

Chapter 20:

The new covenant is better

But now hath he obtained a more excellent ministry, by how much also he is the mediator of a better covenant, which was established upon better promises.

Hebrews 8:6 (KJV)

I once visited an online auction site to find an antique oil painting. It was interesting to see how antiquated, late-sixteenth-century paintings were much more valued and sought after than some recent twentieth-century paintings. I noticed that the older some paintings were, the higher the prices were. A Van Gogh impressionist painting from the nineteenth century would attract more bidders than a modern landscape painting because of the artist's well-established reputation, the age and unique quality of the painting. Because Van Gogh can no longer produce new works, these old paintings have more value than a modern artist's.

Unlike sentimental values derived from an antique painting, today there is no sentiment to be derived from keeping the Law.

Upon the death of Jesus, the old covenant (Law) was fulfilled (Matthew 5:17) and the New covenant was ratified. The Bible is a book containing two major covenants: the Old and New Testaments. The Old reveals how God, in times past, dealt with His people, the nation of Israel, and the New reveals how He relates to people (including us) after the death of His Son; Jesus. How God related to people after the Law was given is completely different to how He relates to us today. Today, God does not treat us according to the old covenant but according to the new. In a comparison between the two, the writer of the book of Hebrews concludes that the new covenant is better than the old (Hebrews 8:6).

Exodus 20 highlights the old covenant and the requirements people were expected to attain in order to receive God's blessing and favour. These requirements were to be completely kept and performed to qualify for God's blessings. A repeating clause in the old covenant was 'thou shall'. This was an agreement predicated on people's presumed ability to do all that the Lord required. God was always gracious to them before its inception, and the Law was given because people presumed they could go on without any need for God. In Exodus 19:8, 'The people all responded together, "We will do everything the Lord has said." So Moses brought their answer back to the Lord.'

Hundreds of years of living under the old covenant only revealed to the people that this agreement was not working. God Himself found fault with it, because the people could not keep its requirements. Hebrews 8:7–8 says, 'For if there had been nothing wrong with that first covenant, no place would have been sought for another. But God found fault with the people and said: "The days are coming, declares the Lord, when I will make a new covenant with the people of Israel and with the people of Judah."

The Law is perfect and holy but the problem and imperfection arose from imperfect people who could not keep its terms. In all the Old Testament, people did not get blessed by keeping God's laws perfectly. People got blessed only because there was a provision God had put in place to bless His people if they offered sacrificial animals for the covering of their sins. The blessings of the Old Testament were received only on the basis of the shedding of blood of sacrificial animals and not obedience to God's Law. Man utterly failed at keeping God's Law but God still blessed them on the basis of a sacrifice.

God made this agreement obsolete by bringing about a new covenant. Today, some believers are updating what is outdated by trying to keep God's Law in order to receive the blessing. Don't employ an outdated system of the Law under this new dispensation of grace. The Law of Moses and the Mosaic covenant are outdated. Hebrews 8:13 says that by calling this covenant 'new', God has made the first one obsolete; and what is obsolete and outdated will soon disappear.

Before the new covenant came into effect, the righteousness of the old had to be fulfilled. The inception of the new was preceded by the fulfilment of the old in Jesus Christ. Only Jesus fulfilled the requirements of God's Law. He fulfilled the old covenant and inaugurated the new covenant. In fulfilling the Law and its requirements, He restored its pristine value, kept it completely to God's perfect standard and then put an end to the old in order to establish the new.

The new compared to the old is completely dependent on God for its fulfilment. The main clause of the new covenant is 'I will'. Unlike the old, where the agreement was between a holy God and sinful people, in the new, God Himself takes full responsibility. The new is between God the Father and His Son, Jesus Christ with the Holy Spirit bearing witness to the covenant.

> But God found fault with the people and said: "The days are coming, declares the Lord, when I will make a new covenant with the people of Israel and with the people of Judah. It will not be like the covenant I made with their ancestors when I took them by the hand to lead them out of Egypt, because they did not remain faithful to my covenant, and I turned away from them, declares the Lord. This is the covenant I will establish with the people of Israel after that time, declares the Lord. I will put my laws in their minds and write them on their hearts. I will be their God, and they will be my people. No longer will they teach their neighbour, or say to one another, 'Know the Lord,' because they will all know me, from the least of them to the greatest. For I will forgive their wickedness and will remember their sins no more." By calling this covenant "new," he has made the first one obsolete; and what is obsolete and outdated will soon disappear.

Hebrews 8:8–13 NIV

Beloved, this is how God deals with us today: 'I will', 'I will' and 'I will'. He has cancelled and put an end to the old covenant, in order to establish the new. The new covenant is now the new normal. God has sworn never to remember our sins because of His Son Jesus and has promised to put His Law in our heart. These Laws are not the Laws in the old covenant. They are the new covenant laws; the law of faith, the royal law of love and the perfect law of liberty. In the new covenant, God has promised to be our God. He has promised not to remember our sins and unrighteous deeds, all because of Jesus. We are no longer required to perform so as to win the favour of God. We are already favoured by God because of our faith in Jesus. Because of Jesus in us, God's Law is effortlessly and unconsciously fulfilled. Because of Jesus in our heart, we can love God and one another, we can boldly approach His throne and are free to be ourselves in His presence. We can also receive by faith all He has for us His children. We fulfil these Laws even without being conscious of it.

There are no auction sites for the old covenant. It is outdated and obsolete. No value is gained in retaining the old or keeping the Law to impress God. Today, the way to impress God is to believe in what Jesus did for us on the cross by His blood. Believe in Him and be conscious of Him, and you will consequently have access to the favour of God.

PRAYER

I am not under the old covenant any more, therefore sin, Satan, sickness and every curse under the Law have no dominion over my life. I am under the new. The royal law of love, the perfect law of liberty and the law of faith all operate effortlessly in my life.

Chapter 21:
One Thing

For it is God who works in you to will and to act in order to fulfil his good purpose.

Philippians 2:13

You have probably heard the saying 'if you fail to plan, you have planned to fail'. I grew up with the mindset of planning my days and weeks so time could be properly managed and not wasted. A daily 'to do' list helped me plan the day and organise my time. With this list, activities and events were set in order of priority and accomplished accordingly.

Coming up with a comprehensive 'to do' list was one thing, but crossing over from 'to do' to 'done' was a different ball game. Sometimes, being a little too ambitious only resulted in zero impetus for getting started on even the smallest of activities on the list.

At the start of every year, many people begin their year with a vision or a New Year's resolution. The dawn of a new year brings the excitement of the unknown mingled with a desire to be or do better than the year before. And so we start the year with great momentum, fuelled with a list of things to do during the course of the year.

- Read 50 books a year
- Learn 100 scriptures a year
- Travel places
- Learn a language
- Save money
- Lose or gain weight
- Join a health and fitness club

On and on the list goes. As great as these ambitions are, a detailed review of my progress towards goals like these at the end of each year used to leave me with a sense of guilt and condemnation for not accomplishing what I had set out to do. I seldom celebrated what I had accomplished, and focused more on the 'half-empty glass'. A glance at the unaccomplished list only revealed my shortcomings and inability to do what I initially set out to do.

In Exodus 19, the children of Israel had just left Egypt and had been set free from bondage and slavery. God brought them out because of his own goodness, not because they were good. When Moses came down the mountain and brought God's Word to them, without listening to the terms of the Law, they prided themselves in their own ability to keep this 'to do list' – the Ten Commandments.

So Moses went back and summoned the elders of the people and set before them all the words the Lord had commanded him to speak. The people all responded together, "We will do everything the Lord has said." So Moses brought their answer back to the Lord.

Exodus 19:7–8

Israel presumed they were able to keep God's Law and needed no help. They invariably told God, 'Moses, go and tell God we can keep the Law completely all by ourselves and we really don't need any help from Him.'

The Law is good and righteous. There is nothing wrong it. It is perfection encapsulated. It revealed God's standards and set out God's expectations of the children of Israel. Its requirements were meant to be adhered to and observed with no room for any imperfection. You either kept it all or broke it all. It was either all or nothing. However, the problem was with the people. Imperfect people given a perfect Law! 'Whatever you require me to do Lord I can do it. I don't need you!' What a statement of pride. What an exaltation of self and the crowning of man's ability over God's grace!

Only a few days later, they broke the very Law they prided themselves on being able to keep and obey! They just couldn't do it without the help and grace of God.

Friend, a 'to do' list is great, a vision book is excellent. Planning and preparing for the future is equally beneficial. God told

Habakkuk to write the vision down and make it plain, so that they who saw it could run with it (Habakkuk 2:1). The key to success and good favour lies in where you place your confidence and trust. Do you think you can do it without God's help? Do you take pride in yourself and trust your experience more than you do God? Are you more confident in your ability to accomplish your plans for your life or are you helplessly and hopelessly dependent on God's grace to help you? Do you count your wealth of resources and your arsenal of contacts more than you do God? God wants us to put our trust and confidence in Him and not in our ability. He wants us to rely on His grace to help us with our daily, weekly or annual plans and events of life. It is His grace that gives us the ability to accomplish all we have set out to do. It is not the 'to do' list that places you over and above in life, but His grace that causes us to do His good pleasure. God wants you to fall in love with a person and not a formula or a principle.

You may be inundated with a thousand and one things to do today, but start with Him. Tell him, 'Father, I thank you because you are with me. With you all things are possible.' Acknowledge His presence in your life before you begin your endeavours. Sit at the feet of Jesus and do the one thing you most need, which is receiving from him as Mary did while she sat at the feet of Jesus (Luke 10:39).

A baby learns to sit up first, before crawling, standing, walking or running. If you want to stand tall, walking and running the race of life, accomplishing all you are set to do, it begins by first sitting at the feet of Jesus. When Jesus visited Mary and Martha, Martha served while her sister Mary sat at the feet of Jesus. As the day went by, one became tired and exhausted and yelled at Jesus, saying 'You don't even care that my sister is not helping!' She got exhausted because she had many things to do; yet she did not do the most important thing.

We may have many things to do. Many calls to make, many targets to reach, many places to go, many visits to make, many deadlines to meet, many exams to pass, but the good news is that there is only one needful thing to do. Others are secondary to this one needful thing. Sit at the feet of Jesus and let Him feed you with His loving and gracious words. Let His grace saturate your life, and then you will be able to do the many other things. Don't get condemned for not being able to accomplish goals you have set out in times past. Instead, look to Jesus and allow His grace to empower you to be all He has called you to be.

PRAYER
Lord Jesus, I sit at Your feet and receive Your grace in abundance. I acknowledge You in all my ways and You will direct my path. I rest in Your grace and receive Your love. Now I'm empowered to do all You have called me to do.

CHAPTER 22:

YOU LOOK AMAZING UNDER THE LIGHT

Arise, shine, for your light has come, and the glory of the LORD rises upon you. See, darkness covers the earth and thick darkness is over the peoples, but the LORD rises upon you and his glory appears over you. Nations will come to your light, and kings to the brightness of your dawn.

Isaiah 60:1–3

I got up early one morning to run. Noticing how dark it was outside, I took along a torch to illuminate the dark patches of my running route. Along the route were streetlights that turned on at a set time during the day. Most were still off when I was running. When I got to an area that was well lit by the streetlights, I turned off my torch until I reached an area with no light, and turned it back on again. A few times, I forgot to turn off the torchlight where the streets were well lit. I hardly noticed any difference my light made because of the strength of the light from the street lamps.

When the streetlights were on, my torchlight made no difference at all. The torch served its purpose best when in a dark patch.

Light is at its best in darkness. The darker it got, the brighter and more visible the torchlight appeared. Darkness only creates a stage for light to shine.

The first thing God created was light. Later on the fourth day, God created the Sun, Moon and the Stars. We have an ecosystem sustained by the magnificence of the sunlight. Plants depend on light to make their food, while animals feed on plants. We feed either on plants, animals or both. We can't overemphasise the importance of the sunlight to our world. We are kept warm by the light emitted by the sun and we don't walk around in darkness. If the earth were a little closer to the sun, it would be too hot to sustain life. A few miles further away from the sun, and we would all freeze. To receive the benefits of the sun and its light, God placed the earth exactly where it is.

We are the light of the world today and God has placed us here on earth to reveal His glory and display His goodness. Just as plants and animals are sustained by the light from the sun, the world should be blessed by the light of our God shining in and through us. Those who don't yet believe should be attracted to the Lord Jesus by the brightness of our shining.

Before I got married, I went to a jewellery shop to choose a ring for my wife, Bakang. One of the things the jeweller did was to put the ring under a dark cloth and shine a powerful light source to the ring. Under the light, the diamond looks beautiful. The light reveals the different hues and brilliance of the diamond. When God shines His light on us, His light is not to expose our frailty and leave us condemned. His light is to reveal how beautiful we are in Christ. So instead of running away from the light, run to it and let it reveal how amazing and beautiful a person you are in Christ.

Do you feel as if it's dark in the world? Darkness cannot overwhelm light. Light always swallows up darkness. You are the light of the world. The light of God shines in you and everywhere you go your light shines brighter. You look amazing under the light, so stay there.

PRAYER
Lord Jesus, You are my light and salvation. There is no darkness in my part. I arise today, for my light has come and God's glory shines upon me.

CHAPTER 23:
GOD NEVER LEAVES YOU IN LIMBO

Christ redeemed us from the curse of the law by becoming a curse for us, for it is written: "Cursed is everyone who is hung on a pole." He redeemed us in order that the blessing given to Abraham might come to the Gentiles through Christ Jesus, so that by faith we might receive the promise of the Spirit.

Galatians 3:13–14

God is the most purposeful being that ever existed. There is nothing insignificant about why He does what He does and how He does what He does. Even when we don't fully understand His plans and reasons behind His actions, there isn't a single thought, word or deed of our God without a purpose. For example, in his Gospel, Matthew the tax collector gives the genealogy of Jesus Christ. He begins with 'This is the genealogy of Jesus the Messiah the son of David, the son of Abraham' (Matthew 1:1). If you carry on reading in the King James Version of the Bible, the next fifteen verses are the 'begat' verses. God is so detailed that He has a purpose for even the 'begats'.

When we were redeemed by the blood of Jesus, God had a purpose for redeeming us. The purpose of our redemption is in order that the blessing given to Abraham might come to the Gentiles through Christ Jesus, so that by faith we might receive the promise of the Spirit.

God redeemed us from the curse of the Law into the blessings of Abraham. He never brings you out of one thing without having something better in mind for you. He brought Israel out of Egypt after a period of 430 years because He had in mind a better place for them – the Promised Land; a land flowing with milk and honey. He brought Israel out into a place of abundance.

David recounted the goodness of God. He said 'You let people ride over our heads; we went through fire and water, but you brought us to a place of abundance' (Psalm 66:12).

God never leaves you in limbo. If you seem to be facing a closed door, it is because God is opening a better door for you. You may have faced a terrible and painful situation. God's will is not for His children to suffer in pain. He always provides a door of escape because He loves you and has something, somebody and somewhere much better for you.

The blessing of Abraham cannot be compared to the curse of the Law. Today, you are no longer under the Law but are now under the blessings of Abraham. So, enjoy all the blessings God has for you.

PRAYER

Father, I receive Your grace to enjoy all the blessings for which Jesus died on the cross on my behalf. I may not understand fully how You do what You do, but I trust You. When one door shuts, it's because you have a better one for me, so I let go of every closed door today and by faith, I walk through every open door You have for me.

Chapter 24:
Add Value to Your Life

If what they vowed is a ceremonially unclean animal, one that is not acceptable as an offering to the Lord, the animal must be presented to the priest, who will judge its quality as good or bad. Whatever value the priest then sets, that is what it will be.

Leviticus 27:11–12

God created people in the Garden of Eden, to multiply, rule and have dominion over all the works of His hands. God's will has always been for His creation to display all that He is. We see this in Genesis, Moses' account of how God created man. God formed man from the dust of the ground and put His breath into him, thus the man became a living soul (Genesis 2:7).

After God formed the animals, God brought them to Adam to see what he would call them. The same creative ability to give life into things was displayed in Adam. The animals and birds were not named by God but Adam.

> *Now the Lord God had formed out of the ground all the wild animals and all the birds in the sky. He brought them to the man to see what he would name them; and whatever the man called each living creature, that was its name.*
>
> **Genesis 2:19**

The cow was called a cow because Adam called it a cow. The pig was called a pig because Adam called it a pig. Adam had the ability to name all the animals, yet this ability is minuscule in comparison to what we have in Christ. The first Adam was a living soul, but the last Adam (Jesus Christ) is a life-giver (1 Corinthians 15:45).

Today we bear the image not of the first Adam but of Jesus Christ. We are life-givers. Whenever and wherever you show up, there is a fountain of life in you that changes everything around you. You have the ability to speak life to a dead situation. You can speak fruitfulness to a barren situation. With this life you have the ability to call things that are not in existence as though they already are. Whatever the priest of the Old Testament estimated as the value of sacrificial animal, that was the value. He determined the value and had the final say as to how much the animal was worth. Today you are not a priest under an inferior covenant but one under a new covenant. Through Jesus, we can offer up sacrifices of praise to God (Hebrews 13:15), because He has made us to be kings and priests who serve our heavenly Father.

As a new covenant priest, your words also carry weight. You can call things that are not as though they are. Your words give life to everything dead around you. Through your words, you add value to your life. What really matters is not people's estimation of you. What counts is God's estimation of you, because whether or not you know it, you are worth the precious blood of Jesus and are as valuable as God's Son.

PRAYER

Thank You Lord Jesus for loving me and washing me from my sins in Your own blood. I am a new covenant priest called to serve You. I speak life into every area of my life. I see myself the same way You see me: as the righteousness of God in Christ. Through the gracious words I speak, I add value to the lives of all those who come in contact with me today.

Chapter 25:

His Presence Makes the Difference

The blessing of the Lord brings wealth, without painful toil for it.

Proverbs 10:22

Often when we read or hear about blessing, we equate it to material possessions. People who think that the blessing is limited to a car, a house or financial stability have a hard time understanding how a person can say he or she is blessed without the acquisition of material possessions. The blessing is not the things we seek, but a Person. The two are mutually exclusive. God wants you to go after the Person and not the things. The irony is that things are automatically designed to follow those who seek Him.

It delights God when His children are blessed. David reveals the heart of a loving God in the well-being of His children. He writes, 'May those who delight in my vindication shout for joy and gladness; may they always say, "The Lord be exalted, who delights in the well-being of his servant"' (Psalm 35:27). It is God's greatest delight to see His children blessed.

As a father, when my children are sick, I feel so much for them that I am moved to help them feel better in any way I can. If we as earthly parents want the best for our children's health, how much more does our heavenly Father want this for us? A God who is bent on punishing His children with sickness, disease, pain or lack is the complete antithesis of the God of the Bible. God's disposition is to see us blessed.

Joseph was sold into slavery and yet was successful. It sounds like an oxymoron. A successful slave. How can one be a slave yet be successful? How can one be in lack or want and yet be blessed? How can one be diagnosed with a life-threatening disease and yet be healed? The answer to these questions is seen in Genesis 39:2: 'The Lord was with Joseph so that he prospered, and he lived in the house of his Egyptian master.'

The blessing of the Lord is not seen in *what* you have but *who* you have. Physically, Joseph had nothing. As a slave he was probably sold naked on the auction block, but even in this state of not having anything, he had everything because the Lord was with him. Joseph started off with nothing, but God's presence in his life lifted him to a place where he had everything. He was put in charge of Potiphar's house. When thrust into prison because of Potiphar's wife's accusations, there he became the prisoner in charge. God later made him prime minister of Egypt.

Today, because the Lord is with you, you are blessed. You are successful and have everything. The presence of the Lord in your life makes all the difference. The blessing is not a thing but a

Person. Jesus is God's blessing to you and with Him you have all things. You are complete and whole, lacking nothing. You may be starting from nothing today, but the good news is that you have everything. It may be a negative diagnosis of a disease you received from your doctor. The good news is Jesus the healer is with you and for you. The presence of Jesus in your life makes everything beautiful. Sickness and disease has to bow its knee to the lordship of Jesus. His presence makes the difference.

PRAYER

Today, I am complete in You. Your presence in my life makes all the difference. I shout for joy and I am glad because You delight in my well-being. Just as You were with Joseph, Father I know that You are with me now, therefore I am successful in all my dealings.

Chapter 26:
God is not put off by our sin

For you know that it was not with perishable things such as silver or gold that you were redeemed from the empty way of life handed down to you from your ancestors, but with the precious blood of Christ, a lamb without blemish or defect.
1 Peter 1:18–19

The price of a commodity or service is reflected in its value or worth. The amount you are prepared to pay for a good or service is determined by its quality, quantity and value.

The significant differences between Rolex and Ralex watches are not only seen in their spellings but also in the price tags attached to each product. One can be picked up for a few pounds, but the other will cost thousands more. The difference in price is not only due to the branding of the watches but their quality and value.

When God wanted to buy us from the slavery of sin and the condemnation of the Law, He looked around to see if there was anything as valuable as the ones to be redeemed. No amount of gold or silver could pay for our souls. No amount of money could stand in comparison to the value He placed on us. The only price that could pay for our redemption was the precious blood of His Son. It took the death of Jesus Christ to redeem us from our sins. That's how valuable you are to God. You are a man of great substance and a woman of great worth.

Your price is worth more than silver or gold, far more than rubies. God sees you as precious. How do you see yourself? In God's eyes, you are precious. You are worth something. You are the apple of His eye and the object of His delight because of Jesus. In fact you are worth so much that He gave the greatest and most treasured possession He had for our redemption. He gave everything – Jesus.

We were so precious to God *before* we were saved, that He was not put off by our sins and inability to keep His holy Law, but sent His Son to redeem us. Now that we are saved and redeemed, now that we belong to Him, how much *more* valuable are we to Him because of His precious Son Jesus Christ?

> *For if, while we were God's enemies, we were reconciled to him through the death of his Son, how much more, having been reconciled, shall we be saved through his life!*
> **Romans 5:10**

Today, you are so precious to God who gave everything to redeem you. God sees you through the lens of the precious blood of Jesus. You are precious to Him. See yourself that way. If

God gave us everything, by sending His Son Jesus when we were nothing but sinners, now that we are redeemed, righteous and precious there is nothing He will withhold from us because of His Son.

PRAYER

I am precious to God. I am a person of great worth and value. I am accepted by God and I am His beloved. The precious blood of Jesus was paid for my redemption. Jesus' blood makes me precious. I know who I am in Christ. I am the righteousness of God in Christ.

Chapter 27:

Accessing the Promises of God

It was not through the law that Abraham and his offspring received the promise that he would be heir of the world, but through the righteousness that comes by faith.
Romans 4:13

God means every word He says and says every word He means. God loves to see His children walk in the reality of all His promises. God was so serious about bringing to pass what He promised Abraham that He made a covenant with him. Through Jesus Christ, today we are Abraham's offspring and have access to the same promises.

Whenever a promise is made to someone, the fulfilment of the promises hinges on the one who made the promise. If I promise to give you a sum of money as a gift by a specific date, then the fulfilment of the promise depends on my ability to do what I promised. For me not to give you what I promised at the specified time only tarnishes my image and brings to bear questions about the authenticity of my words. The next time I make you a promise, you will not only question my ability to perform, but may doubt me because of my failure to deliver on my previous promise.

What makes God trustworthy and dependable is that He has never failed to execute what He promised. God always brings to pass every one of His promises. When He made a promise to Abraham, the fulfilment of such promise did not depend on Abraham, it completely depended on God. All Abraham was required to do was to believe in the One who made the promise.

I am often asked about how to receive all of God's promises. The answer is to understand that God's promises are a gift. They are unconditional and only require our trust and confidence in the ability of the One who promised.

When God promised Abraham a son, there were no laws or requirements for Abraham to keep for the fulfilment of the promise. The laws of God given to Moses in the Ten Commandments only came about 430 years after God made Abraham a promise. Yet Abraham received all that God promised him by faith. Some people have the idea that Abraham worked and performed righteous acts before God to qualify for the promise and may have instigated a course of action for God to bless him with his son Isaac.

Romans 4:19 tells us the physical condition of Abraham and Sarah: without weakening in his faith, he faced the fact that his body was as good as dead since he was about a hundred years old and that Sarah's womb was also dead.

At such an old age, Abraham and Sarah's bodies were infertile. They could not have been responsible for producing the promised son. The promise of Isaac was not because Abraham kept God's commandment or because he performed any righteous deeds. There were no Ten Commandments to keep. The promise was not because of Abraham's effort either. Abraham received the promises of God through the righteousness of faith – by believing God.

The way Abraham received the promises of God is the same way we receive God's promises today. We inherit the promises and all the blessings of Abraham through the righteousness of faith. We don't need to work or perform to receive what is promised. The fulfilment of the promises of God in our lives hinges completely on our Lord and Saviour Jesus Christ. Christ alone kept and fulfilled all of God's Law, and when we believe what He did on the cross, we are righteous and have access to the blessings of God.

Don't ask yourself if you qualify or if you measure up to God's blessing. Ask yourself 'does Jesus qualify? Does Jesus measure up to the promises of God?' The answer is a big yes, and through Him we also have the blessing of God.

PRAYER

Thank You, Jesus, for qualifying me to be a partaker of the blessing of Abraham. I am righteous – not by works, but by faith in Your blood – and because of this, all of God's blessings are mine.

CHAPTER 28:
GRACE MANAGEMENT

Christ redeemed us from the curse of the law by becoming a curse for us, for it is written: "Cursed is everyone who is hung on a pole."

Galatians 3:13

The word 'redeem' is a rich Bible word, meaning to buy up,[5] buy out, or to release by paying a ransom price.[6]

When a property is on the market, a 'for sale' placard is usually put up to attract potential buyers. An interested party calls the agent to inquire further about the property and arrange a viewing. Once this has taken place, if the buyer still wants to proceed, an offer to buy is made to the agent. Once an

---

[5] NT: 1805, *Olive Tree's Enhanced Strong's dictionary and Vine's complete Expository Dictionary of Old and New Testament Words*. Copyright © 2011, Olive Tree Bible Software, Inc.

[6] NT: 3084, *Olive Tree's Enhanced Strong's dictionary and Vine's complete Expository Dictionary of Old and New Testament Words*. Copyright © 2011, Olive Tree Bible Software, Inc.

agreement is made, the property is taken off the market. Upon the exchange of contracts between both parties, a sale is made and there is a change of ownership. The buyer has changed from a position of being interested to being the new owner of the property, because they have bought up – or redeemed – the property. The property is released to the buyer on receipt of payment.

As a result of Adam's disobedience in the Garden of Eden, we were sold into the 'sin' market. However, God so loved the world that He decided to buy us out of the market for Himself. He redeemed us by Jesus dying on the cross for us. We were redeemed by God Himself.

Titus 2:14 shows that God gave Himself in the person of Jesus to redeem us to Himself: 'who gave himself for us to redeem us from all wickedness and to purify for himself a people that are his very own, eager to do what is good.'

Once contracts have been exchanged, the new owner of the property is responsible for the management and care of the property. If the roof is leaking, or maybe there is a crack in the wall, the owner of the property is responsible for the maintenance and upkeep of the property. It is not the responsibility of the property to fix itself. The building, left by itself with no attention, will eventually turn into rubble.

Now that we have been redeemed by the precious blood of Jesus, we belong to Him. We are no longer under the dominion of Satan, Sin or the Law. We are now under new management and our heavenly Father has assumed full responsibility for our lives. Our management is grace. We are under grace (see Romans 6:14).

If we are sick in our bodies, Jesus is responsible for our healing. If you have a broken relationship with a child or a loved one, it is now Jesus' responsibility to take care of that. In and of ourselves, we are nothing and can do nothing. But the good news is we are not alone. We belong to Him and our heavenly Father is responsible for every area of our lives. Please understand we still have the responsibility to look after ourselves, but we do so by leaning on His love for us and resting in the assurance that we are His and He will take good care of us. When we put our lives into His hands, He guides us with His Spirit and teaches us how to live and lead a responsible life. His grace in our lives now gives us the wisdom of how to take good care of ourselves, mend broken relationships and lead a life that is pleasing to Him.

PRAYER

I am the redeemed of the Lord. I have been bought with the precious blood of Jesus. My life belongs to Him. Jesus, today I walk in the consciousness of belonging to You. Whatever is wrong, You can make it right and I receive Your grace.

Chapter 29:

Enjoy Good Health

Dear friend, I pray that you may enjoy good health and that all may go well with you, even as your soul is getting along well.

3 John 1:2

I began running in the mornings not because I wanted to, but because I was once in a hard-pressed place financially. Having graduated from university with no money, like many students, I found myself in a place of being without. My first job was to run a local store.

Among the duties were opening and locking up on a daily basis, but I had no means to travel to and from work. There were buses but no means to get a bus fare. Trains ran frequently between my house and work, but there was no money for the ticket. I was so excited about the first job I got and did not want to mess up on day one by not showing up. The lingering question was how to get to work. Do I call in sick? Do I borrow money from friends? Do I postpone my start day? Eventually I came up with a plan: I decided to get up early and run. Five minutes into running, I was exhausted. There was still a distance of about five miles to go. So I paced myself and walked. Catching my breath, I began running again. I did this till I got to work. I was late but still made it. Wiping off the sweat that dripped down my face, I rolled up my sleeves and got on with work. I did the same thing returning home. On day two, I left home a little earlier to avoid getting to work late. Thereafter, I ran every day, and after a couple of weeks, I did not get as tired as I did when I first started out.

When payday arrived, I had enough money to buy a bus ticket. It was an exciting time. However, I did not drop the habit of running. Almost 12 years later, I still run most mornings. Here is the point: the habit of running did not begin because I was passionate about keeping fit. Neither did I start running to get into the discipline of the mind, body and soul. I started running because I was broke and could not even afford a bus fare.

In the process of exercising, fitness may be gained, but this is not the only key to being healthy. Exercise may bring about fitness, but divine health comes from the Lord. There are lots of benefits to looking after ourselves (see 1 Timothy 4:8), but it is the Lord who keeps our souls amongst the living.

Yes, we take care of our bodies because they are God's gift to us. We eat well, rest well and exercise well. Nonetheless, our confidence should not be in our ability to take care of ourselves. Our confidence should be in the Lord. Only He is able to keep and preserve our lives.

Moses lived 120 years on earth. At this age he was strong and his eyes were not dimmed. The secret to his life is found in Hebrews 11:27: 'By faith he left Egypt, not fearing the king's anger; he persevered because he saw him who is invisible.' His life was preserved to a good old age because he kept his focus on God. He continued strong because he acknowledged the presence of God in his life. Longevity, health and healing come from the Lord. Just like parents want their children to be healthy, our heavenly Father wants us healthy and strong. As we keep our eyes on Him and fix our confidence on Him, His healing flows into our bodies and preserves us from any malady.

PRAYER

Lord, I ask that I will live long and strong, that my strength will not fail me and my natural force will not wane. As You keep my mind on Jesus, He is able to keep me in perfect peace. Divine health is Your will for my life. I look to the cross today and see all my sicknesses and diseases nailed to the cross. I am forever young and strong. Forever healthy.

Chapter 30:

Milk versus meat

Anyone who lives on milk, being still an infant, is not acquainted with the teaching about righteousness. But solid food is for the mature, who by constant use have trained themselves to distinguish good from evil.

Hebrews 5:13–14

It is well documented that the milk from the healthy mother of a baby contains all the nutrients required to keep the baby healthy too. God's wisdom is so amazing that every vitamin and mineral essential to the growth and development of the baby is contained in the milk. As the baby grows, they are weaned on to eating solids.

When the children of Israel came out of Egypt, they became hungry and as usual they complained to Moses and Aaron. God was so gracious, He heard their complaints and provided food for them. From heaven, six out of seven days, He sent them bread and meat, which sustained them daily. Throughout their journey of 40 years in the wilderness, God provided them with their daily food. It is very interesting how they ate the same food for forty years and were healthy. There is no recorded case of malnutrition. Every nutrient needed for their growth and development was contained in the food God provided until they got into the Promised Land.

God wants us to have the same desire for His Word as a newborn baby has for milk. 'As newborn babes, desire the sincere milk of the word, that ye may grow thereby' (1 Peter 2:2 KJV). We are to have an unquenchable thirst and insatiable hunger for the Word of God, just like a newborn baby desires to be fed almost every minute. In the Word of God is every nutrient required for our development and growth. The Word is so nutritious that Jesus said 'man shall not live by bread alone but by every word that proceeds out of the mouth of the Lord' (Matthew 4:4). Indeed, God's Word contains the nutrients required for our healing, wholeness, peace, joy and strength for daily living.

There is a difference between desire and diet. Our desire for the Word should be like that of a baby, but our diet is meat (solid food). As believers, the quickest way to grow and develop into maturity is to feed on meat. 'What then is meat?' you may ask. The writer to the Hebrews tells us that meat is the teaching about righteousness. Righteousness is not something we do but it is a gift received. It is not achieved by deeds but received as a gift. God's inheritance is not reserved for babies but for those who feed on the teaching of righteousness and God's grace. We mature to receive the fullness of this inheritance when we understand that there is nothing we can do to qualify for God's favour. There is no act or noble deed displayed on our part that can give us right standing with God and cause us to receive His blessings. We qualify for God's blessing only because of Jesus. We receive the fullness of our inheritance knowing that we are righteous by faith and not by works. Our diet is the gift of our Lord Jesus Christ – He is our righteousness.

PRAYER

Thank You, Abba Father, that the Holy Spirit causes me to desire Your Word like a baby. I delight daily in Your Word. Even right now, as I feed on Your Word, especially on the teachings of righteousness, I receive this gift of righteousness by faith and have access to all the blessings of Abraham.

Chapter 31:

Grace-Directed Activity

For I am the least of the apostles and do not even deserve to be called an apostle, because I persecuted the church of God. But by the grace of God I am what I am, and his grace to me was not without effect. No, I worked harder than all of them – yet not I, but the grace of God that was with me.
1 Corinthians 15:9–10

A car without an engine goes nowhere. However, one with a perfectly functioning engine takes you wherever you desire. The engine gives power to the car and may be described as the source of power to the vehicle. The grace of God produces the power the believer needs to live an extraordinary life. Grace is not an empowerment but produces an empowerment. Grace is unearned, unmerited, undeserved favour that can only be received as a gift by believing in Jesus and His perfect sacrifice on the cross. Once received, the grace of God now becomes the powerhouse that drives the believer. Grace produces an empowerment to live a righteous, holy and powerful life. Grace produces in us the ability to do things that are pleasing to God. Grace qualifies the disqualified and empowers the powerless.

Grace unlocks doors for those who are completely dependent on God.

The apostle Paul knew what it meant to receive the grace of God and live a life of grace. Here is a man who by all counts of human estimation is disqualified to be used by God. Remember his résumé: a Pharisee and the son of a Pharisee, steeped in the laws of the Jews, taught by the best teachers and professors of his days, zealous and passionate about persecuting the church. Yet God choose him to be the greatest expositor of this amazing gospel of grace.

The grace of God is not a licence to be lazy. The grace of God, once received, now empowers us to work. It is an outworking of an inward gift. The grace of God works in and through us. Under this new covenant, we labour and work but the source of power and drive comes from God. Hebrews 4:11 tells us we labour to enter into rest. Instead of operating from a place of stress and being demand-conscious, now that we are under grace, we rest in the arms of our Saviour and let His grace direct all our activities. It is one thing to worry about meeting the demands of life from our limited resources, but it is another thing to rest in the unlimited supply of God's grace and allow His grace work through you to meet every demand of life.

Let's take a scenario of someone in need of employment. People living under grace don't stay at home sleeping all day, they don't spend time loafing in wait for a surprise knock on their door with a message from an employer saying, 'We've got a job for you!' Equally, grace people don't go to the other extreme of worry or stress about their daily requirements being met. They are always in the flow of this consciousness: 'I can do all things through Christ who strengthens me.' They approach every situation with a consciousness that God's favour is on their lives and He has already made a way. Even when they face adversity and rejection, when things don't go according to their plan and turn out to be a setback or a disappointment, they pick themselves up, knowing that God will always cause them to triumph.

Under grace people don't live lascivious lives, no, never! God's grace in us teaches us to deny sin and embrace righteousness (Titus 2:11). Grace people go the extra mile to help others more, and are a blessing to others. They go beyond the call of duty and are refreshed to go further because the driving force behind all they do is grace. We are people under grace!

Prayer
Thank you, Father, for Your grace. Today I am equal to every challenge I may face. Your grace empowers me to overcome and live a victorious life. I receive Your grace.

Chapter 32:

Astronomical Progress

Then they were willing to take him into the boat, and immediately the boat reached the shore where they were heading.

John 6:21

One step forward and two steps backwards. Do you feel like you are in motion, burning and expending energy but going nowhere? You put so much into an endeavour only to get little or nothing in return?

The disciples of Jesus had experienced a first-hand miracle of Jesus – the feeding of the 5,000 – and then Jesus sent them away while He went up to the mountaintop to pray. Nine hours later, as the disciples rowed their boat across the sea, they had only covered a distance of three miles because the inclement weather delayed their journey. With such a short distance covered, they could still see Jesus from afar. The disciples welcomed Him into their boat and immediately they arrived at their destination.

What do you do when an outer force beyond your control is bent on restricting your progress in life? The disciples had no control over the rough winds that came against them. All they could do was welcome Jesus. You may not have any say in the direction of the winds that blow into your life, but you do have the choice of welcoming Jesus into your boat. The moment you do, all wind ceases because He has the power to calm the storms. Things begin to work in your favour and you make astronomical progress with Jesus in your boat. The moment the disciples received Jesus, that was the very moment they completed their journey and reached their destination. The remaining distance of about seven miles was completed in a split second.

This reminds me of the very first miracle Jesus performed in Galilee. It was a marriage ceremony and they had run out of wine. Jesus asked His disciples to fill six water jars with water. The disciples obeyed and Jesus asked them to draw some out and give to the governor of the feast. On tasting the wine, the governor of the feast called for the bridegroom and gave him the credit for keeping the best wine for later. In this case Jesus performed a 'two-in-one' miracle. Not only was water turned into wine, but good wine was also made in record time! Normally it takes five to ten years to make a good vintage wine: growing the vine, harvesting the grapes, then crushing and fermenting them. Jesus compressed time and made happen in a split second what should ordinarily take the best part of ten years.

Jesus has the power to restore or create in an instant things that would naturally take years. You may ask how, but friend, that's not your part. Our part is not to figure out how or when or who He'll use to get the job done. Our part is to believe. His part is to work. Our part is to rest. The more we trust Him and rest in His ability, the more we see His power at work in our lives.

You will not spend the rest of your years in obscurity, battling against the forces of life that are set to come against you. There is enough grace in you to calm your storms, quiet every raging sea and get you to the place of your destiny. A day with the Lord is like a thousand years and a thousand years is like one day. The good news is that Jesus is in your boat. He is in your heart and can restore all your lost time and wasted years. So did the children of Israel experience restoration as they came out of Egypt. In one night they became millionaires. Not only three million people came out of Egypt but three million millionaires came out of Egypt (see Exodus 12:35–36). God restored their fortune in one night. The same God can do this for you. The key is trusting His grace and not becoming bound up in what we can or cannot do. We rely helplessly and hopelessly on His ability and in no time you will hear the breakthrough beat at your door.

PRAYER
The storms may blow and the tide may roar. Yet You are my hope, my refuge and my hiding place.
I lean on You, Jesus, I draw near to You. I put You in the midst of every storm and fix my eyes on You. Jesus, with You in my life, all things are made perfect. This I know: it is well with my soul.

CHAPTER 33:
ANOINTED WITH OIL

You prepare a table before me in the presence of my enemies. You anoint my head with oil; my cup overflows. Surely your goodness and love will follow me all the days of my life, and I will dwell in the house of the Lord forever.

Psalm 23:5–6

As a kid, my dad had a dream for me to become a medical doctor. What an ambitious vision a parent had for a kid! God had a better plan though: for me to become a preacher of the gospel of grace. As parents, God has given us the awesome privilege of raising our children. When He gives children, He sees in us the qualities fit for receiving such little ones into this world and grants us the wisdom and ability to raise them. Sometimes as parents, in our quest to have our children live to their full potential, we struggle between the thin line of having them fulfil our desires and having them fulfil God's desires. God, who gave them to you, is also able to reveal the purpose of their lives and what they were born to do if we ask and trust His guidance.

In the Old Testament, mothers had great desires for their children, especially sons. They wanted their sons to be prophets, priests or kings, because the prophesied Messiah would come from their midst. Then, the greatest pride of a parent would be to see their children work as a prophet, priest or king.

What was so special about these three roles that made them the desire of parents in the Old Testament? The prophets were God's spokespeople to His people. God revealed His mind to His people through the prophets. They represented God to them. The priests had a different role: they represented the people to God. The kings served in the office of a judge and were required to deliver the people from bondage to their enemies. All three offices were a type and a shadow of our Lord Jesus Christ. He is our prophet, priest and king.

Before entering into such offices, the prophet, priest and king had to be anointed with the anointing oil. David was anointed as king, Aaron was anointed as a priest and Samuel was anointed as a judge and prophet. The anointing oil represented God's choice to His people. Oil on the head meant the one anointed was favoured by God and placed into one of these three privileged offices, because anointing oil was only reserved for the prophets, priests and kings.

But in Leviticus, we see an exception to this rule when it came to the cleansing of the leper. The priest was not only required to anoint the ear, thumb and toe of the leper but to pour oil on the head.

> *And of the rest of the oil that is in his hand shall the priest put upon the tip of the right ear of him that is to be cleansed, and upon the thumb of his right hand, and upon the great toe of his right foot, upon the blood of the trespass offering.*
>
> **Leviticus 14:17**

According to Levitical law, the unclean leper was kept away from the people, outside the camp, because whoever touched the leper became unclean. However, God graciously made provision in the old covenant that during the examination or cleansing of a leper, they were to be anointed with oil. The same oil used for prophets, priests and kings was now to be put on a leper. Through the oil it seems the leper who was meant to be disqualified from being among the people now qualified to be in the same position as the prophets, priests and kings. Oil on anyone, whether a leper or a king, meant the favour, blessing and grace of God was on that person. This was a vivid demonstration of God's grace in qualifying the disqualified. The oil made it possible for the leper to receive the same blessing of the prophet, priest or king.

Because of Adam, sin entered into the world. We were born after the image of Adam, as sinners into the world. We were once like the leper, cut off from the promises and the blessing of God. But because of the blood of Jesus, we now are raised up together and qualify to sit together with Christ in heavenly places. This is the uplifting and empowering ability of God's grace. This unearned, unmerited, undeserved favour now produces the blessing of God in our lives and we now qualify to sit with Jesus far above principalities and powers.

Today, because of the blood of Jesus, you are no longer a sinner but the righteousness of God in Christ. You are in the best place to be desired. You are seated together with Christ.

Prayer

Thank You, Lord, that I am seated together with Christ in the heavenly places. I qualify to be a partaker of this inheritance: because of Jesus I am the righteousness of God in Christ.

Chapter 34:
Pull Out Your Receipt

Christ redeemed us from the curse of the law by becoming a curse for us, for it is written: "Cursed is everyone who is hung on a pole."

Galatians 3:13

During special seasons and occasions, such as Christmas, New Year or birthdays, we intentionally appreciate the people who are dear to us. We exchange pleasantries and kind words: 'Happy birthday!' or 'Happy New Year!' or 'I love you, darling'. Sometimes we celebrate by giving and receiving gifts, presents, cards or gift cards. We get taken out for meals, go to the movies, take a break or do something that engages us with our loved ones.

Last year, one of my Christmas presents was a gift card. A couple of months later, my wife and I went shopping and we bought her a pair of shoes. I used the gift card I had received as a present to pay for them. The language used to describe the transaction was redeeming the gift card for a pair of shoes. To redeem means to do business in a marketplace, to buy or sell.[7] Once an item has been paid for or redeemed, it belongs to the one who made the payment.

On the cross of Calvary, Jesus Christ redeemed us from the Law and all its curses. Man has never kept, and can never keep, all of God's Law. As a composite whole, God's laws are required to be kept completely. 'For whoever keeps the whole law and yet stumbles at just one point is guilty of breaking all of it' (James 2:10). As a result of not being able to keep all of God's Law to meet its righteous requirement, we were condemned and subject to the curse of the Law. Deuteronomy 28:15–68 spells out all that we have been redeemed from. Categorically, we have been redeemed from sicknesses and diseases, we have been redeemed from poverty and lack, and we have been redeemed from death.

We are not subject to the Law and its curses any more, because we are no longer under it. Jesus Christ of Nazareth paid for our redemption with the price of His own blood and the payment for this transaction was made to God. We have been delivered from the Law and its curses and now belong to God. Sickness, poverty and death have no right over your body because a complete payment for your redemption has been made.

---

[7] NT: 0059, *Vine's complete Expository dictionary of Old and New Testament words*, 1984. Nashville Tennessee: Thomas Nelson.

Let's imagine that on my way out of the store, I get spot-checked by a security officer. The receipt I received serves to prove not only that a payment has been made, but that I am now the rightful owner of the shoes. I don't have to cry or accuse the security officer for stopping me. I don't have to complain about why he picked on me from a crowd of a thousand others for a random check. All I need to do is reach for the receipt to show payment has been made.

The same should be our response when sickness comes knocking on your door, we don't have to cry or complain about the sickness to the devil. No! Simply pull out the receipt. Your receipt is the redemptive work Jesus did on the cross after which He cried out with a loud voice 'It is finished'. So when sickness shows up, pull out the Word of God, which is proof that the payment for sickness has been made on the cross, and declare, 'by His stripes I am healed' (Isaiah 53:5). When lack or poverty raises its ugly head at you, pull out the receipt that says 'my God shall supply all my needs according to His riches in glory by Christ Jesus' (Philippians 4:19). When the spirit of death tries to steal your life, pull out your receipt that says 'with long life He will satisfy me and show me His great salvation' (Psalm 91:16).

Prayer

I am redeemed. I've been bought with the precious blood of Jesus. Lord Jesus, Your blood sets me free from the curse of the Law, guilt and condemnation. I am no longer my own. I have been bought with Your precious blood and I belong to You. I have the blessing of Abraham. I am justified by faith.

Chapter 35:

You've Been Upgraded to First Class

When men are cast down, then thou shalt say, There is lifting up; and he shall save the humble person.

Job 22:29 (KJV)

I rushed out of my office and dashed for the train station after preaching on a Sunday morning. A good friend agreed to give me a lift in his car. My train was leaving for the airport in twenty minutes and I had no time to get there. Drawing closer to the train station, I realised my wallet that contained my train tickets and bank cards were on my table. If I returned to get them, I would miss my flight and so I continued to the train station without the ticket or wallet. I was allowed to board the train by presenting an email showing confirmation of my booking.

I got to the airport on time and boarded a plane to the continent of Asia. What a great journey it was to Asia. There, I experienced God's amazing grace.

On returning to the UK, I got to the station but this time was not allowed to board the train without a ticket. The confirmation email was irrelevant and I was asked by the gate attendant to go and make a new purchase from the ticket office.

As I got to the ticket office, I met a gentleman named Tim, who asked what tickets I wanted to buy. I explained to Tim how I rushed, having finished preaching at church and forgot my wallet on my table. He asked me to wait a minute, went to the backroom and came back with a piece of paper in his hands. He said, 'I'm not a Christian, but I hope this can make the world a better place.' He then handed me the piece of paper and said 'You've been upgraded to first class on the next train.' I was stunned and lost for words. My mouth looked like a flytrap for a moment, as I just simply said nothing. Finally, I thanked him for his generosity, got on the train and sat in the first-class carriage. It was a journey well cushioned, with comfort and class. Never had I experienced the pleasure and delight of sitting in the first-class carriage of a train, but there I was. I sat there in awe of what God had just done. I said repeatedly to myself under my breath, 'Thank You Jesus, I am the disciple whom Jesus loves'.

A few minutes into the journey, a lady with two pots in her hands said 'How may I serve you? Tea or coffee?' I thought, 'You left your wallet at home so you'd better pass up and ask for nothing. You can't pay'. I hesitantly replied 'Tea, please'. Pouring out the tea with joy she looked at me and said 'Anything else?' I responded, 'Oh yes please. I'd like some biscuits too.' I was given everything I requested and was well taken care of on that train.
The customer service was just splendid. It was as if God had saved the best for last and crowned my journey with an upgrade

to first class on the train. I did not pay a penny to get on the train, to sit in first class or to enjoy the food and service. The food and drink were all covered as part of the treatment received in first class.

This experience sums up what Jesus did on the cross of Calvary for us. As a result of man's sin in the garden, we were lost and needed salvation. We were spiritually bankrupt; there was no way Adam could redeem himself. Jesus paid the price for us through His blood shed on the cross. His blood now gives us access to experience the first-class treatment of God. God is not punishing or judging you today for your sins or wrongdoing. He loves and cares so much for you because one man paid the price in full. You don't have to work to earn your salvation, it's been paid in full on the cross. You don't have to pay for your sins, Jesus did it all. All that is left to do is for us to believe and receive the gift He died to give us, so we can sit, relax and enjoy all of God's blessings. The price on the cross was paid for our sins as well as every blessing of God. We have access to the unmerited favour and grace of the Father.

PRAYER
Father, I receive Your grace today. I have the favour of God flowing in my life. I am the disciple whom Jesus loves and I am conscious of this.

CHAPTER 36:
LOOKING FOR A JOB?

Though thy beginning was small, yet thy latter end should greatly increase.

Job 8:7 (KJV)

Having graduated from a prestigious university with a bachelor's degree in engineering, I decided to go the extra mile by enrolling onto a postgraduate degree. Of course it was a demanding time, as I had to balance church life with my studies, but God's grace was sufficient to see me through.

I was so proud and privileged to complete a Master's in medical engineering and to submit my dissertation, 'The use of atomic force microscopy to determine the physical and mechanical properties of hydrogel'.

I was deluded to think that the more educated I was, the better my chances of getting the best job offers would be. Little did I know how wrong I was until I went through hundreds of emails and letters of rejection all stating the same thing: 'thank you for applying, sorry, but no.'

One day, after countless disappointing letters of rejection, I got one letter in the post that read something like this:

> *Thank you very much for sending your résumé. We are very impressed with your qualifications and the skills you highlighted in your application. We are pleased to let you know that among the candidates considered for this role, your application was shortlisted. However, due to your lack of experience, we will not be taking your application any further.*

I read this letter over a hundred times because I thought if I came this close and still did not get the job, what chance did I have of getting one?

I was applying for a role in line with what I studied. But employers were more concerned about the skilled experience than the paper qualification. While believing God for a 'real' job, one that related to what I had studied, I ended up doing a temporary job just to make ends meet. I found myself working in a post and print centre. Posting mail, packing boxes, dealing with difficult customers, printing documents, sticking stamps on envelopes, etc. There was nothing wrong with this job, but it wasn't what I expected to be doing at this point in my life. I had spent almost six years in university education, and now I was sticking stamps on to envelopes and leafleting on the high street.

Do you find yourself there? In a place where you never thought you would be, doing things you never dreamt of doing just to make ends meet? Are you at a point of stagnation in business or ministry? Your client base is diminishing and your congregation is not growing. Well there is good news for you today. The Lord is with you right where you are and He has promised never to forsake you. He has already gone before you and is making everything beautiful in your life.

One thing I realised in hindsight was that I trusted my degree to get the job of my dreams. I was confident in the engineering degree and not God. It is not an education degree or the lack of it that gives success in life. It is the presence and the favour of God in your life. Whilst working at the post and print centre, I learnt how to meet deadlines and sales figures. I learnt how to deal with difficult people because we had a business ethic that the customers always came first. This indeed was my small beginning. I certainly learned that a qualification does not guarantee you the job of your dreams.

Having worked there for over a year, I decided to apply for something else within the field of my degree. God opened a door and I had my first professional job. During the interview for the position, I was asked how I dealt with difficult people. Based on the countless experiences from the previous job, it took me no time to come up with an example. I did not have to fabricate one. It came out so succinctly from my lips. I was given the job and this was my first entry into the medical devices sales industry. It was the start of greater things God had for me.

From that experience, I learnt a couple of things:

First, not to despise my small beginnings. You may be in a 'dead-end job', but God always has a better plan for your life. The input you have made and the people you have touched will never go unnoticed.

Second, to trust in the Lord because the Lord Himself is our reward. No matter how excellent you are at what you do or what you know, don't put your trust and confidence in yourself. Promotion only comes from the Lord. Trust in the Lord and not your high IQ or postgraduate degree. The Lord is your wisdom and He will make a way.

PRAYER

Lord Jesus, at every point in my life, help me trust You. Today I stop placing my confidence and trust in my ability and myself, and I place them in You. My beginnings may be small, but my latter end shall greatly increase. I trust You.

Chapter 37:
It's My Time of Grace and Favour

There is a time for everything, and a season for every activity under the heavens

Ecclesiastes 3:1

Sitting by a bay window that overlooked a field with different types of trees, I noticed how each tree reflected the different times and seasons of the year. Taking a close look at them, one could tell if it was winter, summer, spring or autumn. At this time of year, there were no colours, no flowers, no leaves, no movement and hardly any birds perched on their branches: signs showing that winter is here!

It wasn't too long ago when the same trees looked totally different. They had so much life; their leaves swayed gleefully in the gentle breeze. The air was filled with the sweet sounds of happy, chirping birds. Green leaves concealed the trunks and branches of the trees. It was simply picturesque. The same trees looked so different during summer.

When Noah came out of the ark, he presented a sacrifice of burnt offering to God. The sacrifice came before God as a sweet-smelling aroma and God made a promise never to destroy creation with a flood again. God went ahead to institute the different seasons of life. This marked the beginning of a cycle of events that still goes on today. 'As long as the earth endures, seedtime and harvest, cold and heat, summer and winter, day and night will never cease' (Genesis 8:22).

Noah's sacrifice was pleasing and acceptable to God. Following the sacrifice, God made a promise and created the different seasons. Today, Jesus is pleasing to God in every way. He is the perfect sacrifice, that is sweet-smelling to God (Ephesians 5:2), and because of His death on the cross of Calvary, God has promised never to be angry with you and has instituted a perpetual cycle of His favour, blessings and grace for you.

We go through different seasons in our lives. Just like the trees, we adapt to the changes in the seasons. You may be in the winter of life, a time when things feel cold and perhaps slow. No season is designed to last forever; they come and go. Seasons fade in comparison to God's constant supply of grace and favour. Unlike the seasons of life, God's grace never ends; it never runs dry. He has an unending supply of goodness and blessing reserved for you because of the sweet-smelling sacrifice of Jesus.

When asked what time it is, you can happily respond 'it's my time of grace and favour'. Harvest always follows seedtime, just as reaping follows sowing in the fields. God has sown the big seed of His Son, our Lord Jesus Christ. He has reaped and still reaps a harvest of those who put their faith in Jesus. Today you can reap a harvest of favour with God because Jesus, our sacrifice, has been accepted by God.

PRAYER

Heavenly Father, thank You so much for the precious sacrifice of Jesus who is a pleasing, perfect, sweet-smelling sacrifice to You. Today, I enter into an unending season of grace and favour with you. Thank You that You are not angry with me. I have favour with You and because of this, it's always harvest time in my life.

Chapter 38:
Made in His image

Then God said, "Let us make mankind in our image, in our likeness, so that they may rule over the fish in the sea and the birds in the sky, over the livestock and all the wild animals, and over all the creatures that move along the ground."
Genesis 1:26

When we look into a mirror, we see a reflection of ourselves. No one has ever seen their real face, however, the image given by the mirror is convincing enough that we draw conclusions as to who we are and what we look like based on its reflection.

In John's Gospel, Jesus is described as the Word. He was in the beginning when God created the heavens and the earth. The same Word is compared to a mirror in James 1:23 'Anyone who listens to the word but does not do what it says is like someone who looks at his face in a mirror.' So on the one hand, Jesus is the Word and on the other hand the Word is a mirror. If we put the two scriptures together, Jesus is the mirror. He indeed is the true reflection and representation of our God who came in human flesh.

Every time we read the Bible and study the Word of Christ, we have the opportunity to see Jesus in the Word. From Genesis to Revelation, Jesus is seen in every page of the Bible. If you want to understand yourself and know who you are, if you want to know your worth and value, the newspapers, magazines or television are not the right places to find your true identity. Thank God for the information and entertainment given by these media, but when it comes to identity and knowing who you are, then God's Word should be consulted. The Word is our true identity, because when we find Jesus in the Word, we find ourselves.

The first question asked in the Old Testament is in Genesis 3:9 'But the Lord God called to the man, "Where are you?"' When we look at the New Testament, the first question we see asked is when the wise men were looking for Jesus in Matthew 2:2 'Where is the one who has been born king of the Jews? We saw his star when it rose and have come to worship him.' The first question in the Old Testament was about Adam (man) but the first in the New Testament is about Jesus. When you find Jesus, you find yourself.

On one occasion, Jesus asked His disciples who people thought He was. They replied, 'Some say John the Baptist; others say Elijah; and still others, Jeremiah or one of the prophets' (Matthew 16:14). So Jesus asked them directly about who He was. Simon Peter answered and said Jesus is 'the Messiah, the Son of the living God'. The next statement from our Saviour's mouth was just amazing. Jesus replied, 'Blessed are you, Simon son of Jonah, for this was not revealed to you by flesh and blood, but by my Father in heaven' (Matthew 16:17).

Simon Peter got a revelation of Jesus. He saw the Word of God, he had an encounter with the person of Jesus by revelation and then Jesus revealed Simon Peter to himself. 'You are Simon, son of Jonah.' When you see Jesus, the Word of God unveiled, you find your reflection and true identity in Him. We are made in His image and after His likeness. That's our true identity. As He is, so are we in this world. Jesus is not sick or depressed. He is seated at the right hand of God the Father, and so are we. Today we are the righteousness of God in Christ and this is our identity.

PRAYER

I am who God says I am. I am made in the image of God and after His likeness. I am the righteousness of God in Christ. I am pleasing to God because Jesus is pleasing to God. I am loved and accepted by the Father because Jesus is loved and accepted by the Father. As He is, so am I in this world.

CHAPTER 39:

HE IS NEVER TOO LATE

So do not worry, saying, 'What shall we eat?' or 'What shall we drink?' or 'What shall we wear?'

Matthew 6:31

The gospel that has revolutionised my life is the gospel of grace. I have had the privilege of listening to and watching an amazing pastor and expositor of this gospel, Pastor Joseph Prince. Every time I do my life is lifted to a higher level. Here is a personal testimony of how we experienced the Lord's provision in our lives just in the nick of time.

Our tenancy agreement was coming to an end and we had just a few weeks to move house. As we were quite settled where we lived, especially with kids at school, we did not want to move out of that area. All the houses that came on the market were immediately taken and we were getting very unsettled about where we would live.

Late on a Friday evening, an advert for a property was posted on a property website. There was no way the house could be viewed over the weekend as the estate agents were closed. So I went into the estate agents' office first thing on Monday morning, only to be disappointed by the news that the property had already been taken. It was now less than two weeks until we needed to move home but nothing was on the horizon. The pressure was on.

A couple of days later, a beautiful four-bedroom house came on the market and we immediately asked to view it. I was told there were seven other people interested in the house and we were all block booked to see the house one after the other, all on the same day. I viewed the house and it was far beyond what we had in mind. It was much bigger, modern and ideally located. I expressed my interest in renting the house and was told a decision would be made once all eight of us had completed our viewings. On pulling out of the driveway after my viewing, my heart sank when the next interested tenant pulled in just behind me. Naturally, he looked more qualified. I thought he was likely to get the house rather than us.

That afternoon, I was listening to a classic message by Pastor Prince called 'Head knowledge vs. heart knowledge'. Pastor Prince said 'Favour is what causes companies to bypass others selling a product with more experience than you, and make them want to buy from you'.[8] As soon as I heard these words, this

---

[8] Joseph Prince, *Head knowledge vs Heart knowledge* (CD Sermon), 5 September 2003. Singapore: Joseph Prince Resources.

settled it for us. The following day, we got a call from the agent to say we were the new tenants of the house.

God cares so much for you, more than you can ever care for yourself. He knows what you need and when you need it and always comes through at the right time. He's never too early or too late. He always shows up on time. You may be at a point in your life where you need a breakthrough. Don't worry, don't stress, God knows how to surround you with His favour and thoroughly furnish all your needs. Our Lord Jesus admonishes us not to worry or carry a care. In Matthew 6:27 He asks, 'Can any one of you by worrying add a single hour to your life?' The answer is no! So today cast your cares on Him. He knows how to surround you with favour and grant your heart's desires.

PRAYER

Jesus, I cast my cares upon You. I choose not to worry or be stressed about anything. If You care for the sparrows of the air and the flowers of the field, You will take good care of me. So I rest knowing that You can be trusted.

Chapter 40:
You're the Real Deal – The Genuine Article

Then Jesus was led by the Spirit into the wilderness to be tempted by the devil.

Matthew 4:1

Jesus went into the wilderness straight after His baptism. In Matthew 3:17 we see the Father expressing His love and greatest delight in His Son as a voice comes down from heaven, saying, 'This is my Son, whom I love; with him I am well pleased.'

One would think that with such a confirmation of the Father's pleasure in His Son, the next events of Jesus' life would be nothing short of spectacular and supernatural. This was indeed to come, but preceded by the devil's temptation. Again, one would think Jesus, upon hearing the audible voice of the Father, would never encounter any trouble. Imagine yourself receiving a word from the Lord Himself. In an audible voice, He tells you how pleased He is with you (by the way, God is already pleased with you because of Jesus). He reminds you of how beloved and highly cherished you are to Him. You would expect the next stage of your life to be as smooth as a summer lake at dawn, simply because the Lord has spoken to you.

Mark 4:15 says that Satan comes to steal the words immediately after the sower sows the seed. When God's Word is sown into our lives, Satan comes to steal the word. He comes with an urgent immediacy to steal, kill and destroy thereby preventing the promises of God from coming to pass in our lives. And so we must guard our hearts with all diligence and not give the devil a foothold.

Our Lord Jesus was baptised, then led into the wilderness to be tempted by the devil. The Bible clearly states where temptation finds its source – Satan. A good question one could ask is 'If, according to James 1:13, God tempts no one with evil, why then is the Spirit leading Jesus to be tempted by the devil? Is there a form of partnership going on here between the devil and the Spirit?' The answer to this is found in the word 'tempted'. The Greek derivative for this word is *peirázō*, which means 'to try, make trial of, test: for the purpose of ascertaining one's quality, thoughts or how a person will behave himself'.[9] This word carries the idea of conducting an experiment to prove a hypothesis or carrying out a trial to ascertain the quality of a product.

When you look at diamond and zirconia, it is difficult to tell which is which merely by looking at them. They both look shiny,

---

[9] NT: 3985, *Olive Tree's Enhanced Strong's dictionary and Vine's complete Expository Dictionary of Old and New Testament Words*. Copyright © 2011, Olive Tree Bible Software, Inc.

lustrous and dazzle under light. However, to separate the two from each other and to reveal which is diamond or zirconia, a blacksmith will test them both by subjecting them to extreme temperatures. He will put them both into the melting pot and set them on fire. The blacksmith is 'trying' or 'tempting' the two stones in order to ascertain which is diamond. The fire or heat allows the blacksmith to distinguish between the two. The heat unravels each material's property. Under intense heat, zirconia melts at around 2600 degrees Celsius, while diamond has a higher melting point of about 4400 degrees Celsius. The heat was employed not as a destructive tool, but simply to ascertain the properties of the materials under test.

Jesus was not tempted with sin the way we are. Temptation results when there is a sinful lust or passion in a person, but Jesus was sinless in His thoughts and actions and every essence of His life displayed the righteousness of God. The temptation of Jesus in the wilderness was a trial to prove that He was the Son of God who had power over temptation, sin and the devil himself. By leading Jesus into the wilderness, the Spirit was not partnering with the devil. The Holy Spirit led Jesus into the wilderness to prove Jesus is the real deal! In the wilderness, when tempted, Jesus knowing He is God's beloved used the Word of God to conquer and defeat the devil.

Do you feel like you are under fire? Are you being attacked in many ways? Sometimes we ask ourselves how we can be going through such a tragedy just after the Lord gave us His Word. Remember, Satan comes to steal the word, and so when you are in a place of great trial, don't allow your thoughts to incite feelings of fear or trepidation. Don't feel guilty or condemned either. Do not think that you have done something wrong in the past and God is now testing you to see if you are still faithful to Him. It is a master plan of Satan to use thoughts of guilt and condemnation to steal God's Word and eventually kill and destroy.

Friend, know that in the midst of the trial, you have enough substance in you not to be consumed or overwhelmed. Christ is in you and He is the hope of glory. The trial has not come to destroy you but prove to the whole world who you are and what you are made of. You are the real deal, you are the genuine article, you are God's beloved because Christ is in you. You will not melt under heat instead you will keep shining and getting brighter, stronger and wiser, because Christ Jesus now lives in you.

PRAYER

Through Christ Jesus, I win, I conquer and I am an overcomer. I am the righteousness of God in Christ and bold as a lion. Thank You Jesus, because You live in me and strengthen me to face the trials and temptations of life. With You, I am more than a conqueror.

Chapter 41:
Nothing is as big as our God

Enter his gates with thanksgiving and his courts with praise; give thanks to him and praise his name. For the Lord is good and his love endures forever; his faithfulness continues through all generations.

Psalm 100:4–5

The size of every problem is relative to the perspective from which the problem is viewed or dealt with. The Shard is the tallest building in London. With a height of over 300 metres, as you look up at it, your breath is taken away in admiration of such a masterstroke of architectural ingenuity. When you are on an aeroplane above the city, it is interesting to note that the same building is nothing but a speck from your higher perspective. In reality the building is still the same size. It has not diminished in magnitude, instead your viewpoint has changed. Similarly, problems that were once monumental and kept you up all night pale into insignificance when viewed from God's perspective.

God wants you to view life through His lens. The blood of Jesus has brought us to equal ground with God Himself. Whenever life overwhelms you, you already have access into God's presence to see things from God's perspective. Don't be overwhelmed by the size of the burden, it can be removed when you view it from God's perspective. Are you standing on the ground of self-confidence, or are you standing on the strong, uplifting, empowering shoulders of our Saviour? Nothing is as big as our God. There is no mountain insurmountable, there is no valley that cannot be lifted up. There is no problem that surpasses His wisdom and there is no situation that is beyond His power.

Take your eyes off the problem and be God-conscious. Rest on His shoulders of strength and lean in to His heart of love. Our God is forever faithful. He has never failed and He won't fail you: He can be trusted. Keep your eyes and mind fastened on His never-ending love, which was displayed on the cross. We have access into His presence by the blood of Jesus, and right there in His presence, everything changes. Even the hills melt like wax in the presence of the Lord.

PRAYER

By the blood of Jesus I have access into Your presence. Today I declare that all problems and situations I face are minute compared to the magnitude of my God. My God is big.

Chapter 42:

Death is Reversed

With long life I will satisfy him and show him my salvation.
Psalm 91:16

God never meant for us to die or experience any tragedy. He never meant for sickness to invade our body and bring about death. A life of pain and trouble isn't God's plan for us. It was never God's intention for people to be subdued by circumstances of life. When God created people in the Garden of Eden, He said 'let them have dominion over all the works of my hands'. From the start, we see God giving humans the power to be in charge of all He created. They were clothed with God's glory, given the breath of life, and placed in a Garden where all they ever needed was already provided.

Humans disobeyed God's instructions concerning the tree of knowledge of good and evil, and when Adam and Eve ate fruit from the tree, their eyes were opened. They became self-conscious and knew they were naked. Then fear crept in, and they hid themselves from God when He called for them. The act of eating from the tree produced self-consciousness, which in turn produced fear and eventually led to death.

God is not the author of death. Death was the consequence of Adam's disobedience. The consequence of death was tied into the decision Adam made by eating of that tree. But thank God today when we eat of the tree of life – Jesus – the natural course of death is reversed.

> *The Lord God made all kinds of trees grow out of the ground – trees that were pleasing to the eye and good for food. In the middle of the garden were the tree of life and the tree of the knowledge of good and evil.*
> **Genesis 2:9**

A lot of us blame Adam and Eve for paying too much attention to the tree of knowledge of good and evil. Today this seems to be the same mistake many believers are making. We major a lot on the tree of the knowledge of good and evil, but hardly talk about the tree of life. We are taught a great deal about the tree of knowledge of good and evil, but there is not such a zest for knowledge about the tree of life. We have heard about the result of eating of the tree of knowledge of good and evil, how about the tree of life?

The next verse gives a vivid description of what else surrounds this tree.

> *A river watering the garden flowed from Eden; from there it was separated into four headwaters.*
> **Genesis 2:10**

There are two clear images in these verses: a tree and a river. They reappear in this beautiful verse in the book of Revelation:

> *Then the angel showed me the river of the water of life, as clear as crystal, flowing from the throne of God and of the Lamb down the middle of the great street of the city. On each side of the river stood the tree of life, bearing twelve crops of fruit, yielding its fruit every month. And the leaves of the tree are for the healing of the nations.*
> **Revelation 22:1–2**

It's amazing to see a river and a tree in both the first and last books of the Bible. Here in the book of Revelation, we see can the tree of life by a river of life. John, the writer of Revelation, gives us a close-up view of this 'tree of life'. We are given the privilege to know what the fruit of this tree is: healing for the nations.

The tree of knowledge of good and evil brought death, but the tree of life brings healing for the nations. Adam and Eve ate of the tree of knowledge of good and evil and immediately became self-conscious. When you eat of the tree of life, you become conscious not of self but of Jesus. He becomes everything to you. His very life, which brings healing to your body, is released as a result of this consciousness. One tree brought death, but the other tree reverses death to bring life.

Eat of this tree, feast on Jesus, feed on Him. Be conscious of Him and His love for you everywhere you go. He is with you. He is the bread of life; He is our life and health to all our body. With Him, sickness, disease and death are reversed into healing, divine health and life everlasting.

Prayer

Thank You Jesus for Your life-giving spirit. Today I am alive in You and death is reversed. Sickness is reversed, disease is reversed. Jesus, You are the bread of life. You are the tree of life and as I feed on You today, You give life and healing to all my flesh.

Chapter 43:

Favour finds me

"The Lord bless you and keep you; the Lord make his face shine on you and be gracious to you; the Lord turn his face toward you and give you peace."
Numbers 6:24–26

Many are called, but few are chosen. What sets an individual apart from a crowd? What causes people to flock to a product and avoid others? Perhaps you might argue that marketing plays a part. In that case, how would you explain Esther, chosen from a crowd amongst many others, or Ruth, who married Boaz?

Some people attribute their success to luck, but as believers we attribute our success to the favour of God. There is such a thing as 'the favour factor'. Favour is what gives you the edge and takes you out from amongst the crowd to excel. Favour is what causes your business to pick up, prosper and outdo other well-established ones. Gentlemen, favour is what causes that lady you like to say yes to you, overlooking others who you think are more qualified and deserving than you (say amen to that). Favour is what causes people you don't know to help you and go the extra mile for you.

Ruth was a Moabite, who according to the Law of God was disqualified from joining the congregation of God. Because of favour, she had the privilege of being the great-grandmother of David, through whom, generations later, came our Lord and Saviour Jesus.

How did this woman move from a place of obscurity after the death of her father-in-law and husband to a place where she is one of only four other women deemed significant enough to be mentioned in the genealogy of Jesus Christ?

The answer is that she was conscious of God's favour – so much so that God caused her to be gleaning in the field of Boaz. This was the most menial of jobs, yet the favour of God turned her worst into His best. God's favour put her in the right place at the right time. Those who confess the favour of God will find themselves in the right place at the right time. They cannot be ignored or overlooked. There is something about a person who is conscious of the favour of God in their lives. It is possible to know about the favour of God yet not be conscious that the favour of God is with you. It is one thing to know about God, but it is a different thing entirely when you are conscious of the presence of God with you. Ruth not only confessed favour but was conscious of it.

Today the favour of God is on your life because of the perfect work of Jesus on the cross. God's face today is shining and smiling on you so you can experience His favour. On the cross Jesus was punished on our account, so that today God can smile on you and His favour you can experience. Favour is grace and grace is favour. It is receiving and not achieving. It is receiving what you don't qualify for.

You may have a thousand and one reasons why you believe you are not qualified to receive God's favour. Ruth did too: she was disqualified, but favour changed her story. You may feel the least qualified for that job position, the least experienced for the contract. Perhaps no one knows who you are, but the masterstroke of God's favour can take you from being a nobody and make a somebody out of you.

PRAYER
I arise and shine, God's light is on me. God's face is smiling and shining on me. The One who started a good work in me is faithful to complete what He started. Favour finds me. Thank You Jesus.

Chapter 44:
Embrace the New and Live a Purpose-Filled Life

> *Now when David had served God's purpose in his own generation, he fell asleep; he was buried with his ancestors and his body decayed.*
>
> **Acts 13:36**

Have you ever wondered what the purpose of life is? The daily routine of sleeping, waking, eating and working can often become mundane and monotonous unless it all ties in to a meaningful and bigger picture beyond self.

The great heroes of faith recorded in the Bible lived meaningful and purpose-filled lives. For example, God used Moses to bring Israel out of Egypt. He chose Abraham to be a prototype of His blessing both to the nation of Israel and to the world at large. Paul was used to unveil such a wonderful revelation of God's grace. With differing personalities and idiosyncrasies, it is amazing to see how every one of them had a specific call of God on their lives.

The purpose of life is not to exist but to live. Living becomes fulfilling when our lives are invested in a cause greater and bigger than ourselves: to serve God's plan in our generation. A fulfilling or purpose-filled life is one that is spent on living out the counsel of God. God says:

> *"For I know the plans I have for you," declares the LORD, "plans to prosper you and not to harm you, plans to give you hope and a future."*
>
> **Jeremiah 29:11**

God's plans for your life will never get you to a place where you are left totally deflated and exhausted for no use. His plans are always good and gracious. Within His plan, you will experience His favour and generosity that constantly renews and refreshes you every day of your life.

Here is where we sometimes go wrong. We come up with a plan and hope God blesses it. Now there is nothing wrong with drawing up a plan for living your life. However, if it is outside the will of God and not in His plan for you, that is a problem. Instead of deciding what to plan for your life, locate yourself in the plans of God. Every plan you come up with that is according to His will, will always be granted. Within the flow of God's plan, any and everything you do becomes successful. The flow begins with a consciousness of God's presence with you. Being conscious of the presence of God translates you from small beginnings to greater latter ends. Like Joseph, success is guaranteed and you become successful in everything you do, as long as you remain in God's will.

What then, you may ask, is the will of God? In Hebrews 10:5–10, the writer says the will of God for Jesus was for Him (Jesus) to put an end to the first covenant – the old covenant which hinged on performance – and to establish the new covenant. The new covenant, in contrast to the old, is not performance driven. The new covenant hinges completely on a person – Jesus – and not rules. God's will was for Jesus to fulfil the old, put an end to it and establish the new. Today, the will of God for us is that we are established in the new covenant. Not a performance-driven relationship with God but a consciousness that everything has already been done through our Lord Jesus Christ, and we are to believe in what He accomplished for us on Calvary's cross.

When we embrace the new covenant and are established in it, we are no longer conscious of the old. We are not demand-minded but are instead supply-minded. Once this unshakeable foundation is established in the heart of the believer, whatever we desire and plan to do or become will only be an outworking of this foundation, which is the grace of God. We can then live a life full of purpose, one that is meaningful, once we are established in the grace of God.

> *It will not be like the covenant I made with their ancestors when I took them by the hand to lead them out of Egypt, because they did not remain faithful to my covenant, and I turned away from them, declares the Lord. This is the*

covenant I will establish with the people of Israel after that time, declares the Lord. I will put my laws in their minds and write them on their hearts. I will be their God, and they will be my people. No longer will they teach their neighbour, or say to one another, 'Know the Lord,' because they will all know me, from the least of them to the greatest. For I will forgive their wickedness and will remember their sins no more. By calling this covenant 'new', he has made the first one obsolete; and what is obsolete and outdated will soon disappear.

Hebrews 8:9–13

PRAYER

Father, I embrace the new covenant. Thank you for the new covenant founded on better promises. This is Your counsel for my life that I am established in grace. Your will is my will and Your desires are my desires. I receive and flow in Your grace for my life.

Chapter 45:

Most Precious to Me

After Job had prayed for his friends, the LORD restored his fortunes and gave him twice as much as he had before.
Job 42:10

It was a Saturday morning, we had just moved house, and we were getting ready to attend the wedding of a lovely couple at their church, about sixty miles away. While getting my little boy into his car seat, I put my wallet, iPad, iPhone, wallet and a bottle of perfume on top of the car, as I needed both hands to strap Joshua into his seat.

We were all set and ready to go. We had less than an hour before the wedding was due to begin and so time was not on our side. Driving as carefully and quickly as I could, I put down my foot on the accelerator when the road was clear of traffic and went hard on the brakes as I came near bends or islands. We drove out of the town, through wide roads and frequently slowed down when we came to an island. Finally, we were joining a major road at a speed of about sixty-five miles an hour when I heard something drop from behind my car. I looked in the rear-view mirror and noticed it was my bottle of perfume that had fallen from the top of the car and smashed into pieces. Then I remembered all the things I had left on the top of the car.

I thought to myself, 'oh dear!' I knew I could order a replacement for everything else with the exception of one thing, my iPad. It had over a thousand hours of messages and sermons written out on the gospel of grace. There were over two hundred sermons that I had spent hours on end writing out and these were the most precious and dear to me. There were also my notes on many sermons by Pastor Joseph Prince. None of these files were backed up. I had not made any copies or duplicates elsewhere. If I lost or damaged the iPad, that was it. Never again was I to recover the work. The other things – my phone numbers, contacts, bank cards and the bottle of perfume – I could easily get back, but not the notes and the time spent.

I said a little prayer in my desperation as I pulled over to the side of the road, bringing the car to a stop. 'Father, please let my iPad still be on the top of the car.' I came out of the car and there it was. Every other thing had fallen off, but my iPad was exactly where I had left it and had not moved an inch. It was not magnetised to the car – there was nothing holding it down except for the hand of the Lord.

Getting back into the car, I turned around to see if my phone and wallet could be retraced. I found my wallet with all my cards scattered in the grass by the roadside, but not the phone, which was later replaced. Now that was a miracle! That was the hand of God on my iPad. Somehow, the iPad got stuck on the car by the hand of God and did not slide down like the other items. To the natural mind this is impossible, but it happened. I experimented later with a paper notebook similar to the shape, weight and size of an iPad. I drove off and in no time it fell from the top of the car. God knows how to do things that blow our minds and even with all human reasoning, we can never completely comprehend how great His acts are. (And today, I have all my work backed up!)

Have you lost anything in your life? God will give you the ability to recover all. Satan attacked Job and all he had. He lost his children, health, wealth and possessions. God preserved his life and caused him to recover double what was stolen from him. As painful as things may be, our God is a God of preservation and restoration. He will keep you and preserve everything that belongs to you. You will also recover all that Satan has stolen from you. He is a God of restitution; He knows how to protect things that are dear to your heart. Trust in His ability and let Him. Don't fight your battles, rest in His grace and you will recover all Satan has stolen from you.

Prayer

Thank You Jesus for restoring all that has been stolen from me. It is the devil who steals, kills and destroys but You came that I might have life and enjoy it to the full. I receive Your restoration and a recovery of everything that has been stolen from me. Your Grace is more than enough.

CHAPTER 46:
THE HAND OF THE LORD

God did this so that, by two unchangeable things in which it is impossible for God to lie, we who have fled to take hold of the hope set before us may be greatly encouraged.
Hebrews 6:18

God cannot lie. It is just impossible for Him to do so. Everything He says comes to pass because He has the ability to call things that are not as though they are. If God should say today is 22 May 1982, the moment He releases the word, we would all be transported back in time to that very day. By contrast, Satan is not only a liar but the father of lies.

Jesus, in a strong reprimand to the Pharisees of His days who did not believe He was sent from God, said to them, 'You belong to your father, the devil, and you want to carry out your father's desires. He was a murderer from the beginning, not holding to the truth, for there is no truth in him. When he lies, he speaks his native language, for he is a liar and the father of lies' (John 8:44). Satan not only lies but he is the progenitor of lies.

Since Satan is a liar, whatever spews out of his mouth is a lie. The opposite of what he says is true. For example, when he says you are sick and dying, know that this is one of his lies. Instead of dwelling on Satan's lies, meditate on God's Word, which is the truth. His Word says you will live and not die (Psalm 117:17). My friend, we will always be presented with the opportunity to live our lives choosing between two realities. The Truth of God's words or the lies of the evil one. The prophet Isaiah asks 'Who has believed our message and to whom has the arm of the Lord been revealed?' (Isaiah 53:1)

The choice is ours to make. When we choose to believe God's Word, the arm of the Lord is revealed in our lives. The arm of God represents His strength and saving power. The arm of the Lord also reveals God's heart for His children. The unfathomable love expressed in God's heart eventually channels through His mighty saving arms, into the lives of His children to whom He displays his never-ceasing ability to save, rescue and deliver.

The hand of the Lord came upon Elijah in 1 Kings 18:46. He outran King Ahab who was well ahead to the entrance of Jezreel. With the hand of the Lord on Elijah, God graced him to overtake the king and got to the destination in time, before the king on foot.

You may not be given the same privilege and advantages as others in life. You may not have an equal start, or perhaps, you may be at a disadvantaged position because of some physical limitations. Take your eyes off your limitations and understand that the hand of the Lord is on your life. What distinguishes you in life is not what you *have* but the *One* whose hand is on you.

When you believe that God is the most loving Father and that He cares so much for you, His power will be demonstrated in your life. The love God has for us is as strong as the hatred He has for anything against His will for our lives. Today, the arm of the Lord will be revealed to you because you choose to believe in the love God has for you. We have a loving Father who always wants to overtake us with His goodness and surpass our expectations. His arms are not too short to deliver and His love is waiting to be lavishly poured on you.

PRAYER
Because Jesus paid for my sins on the cross of Calvary, God's face of favour is always turned towards me. Lord, I have your undivided attention and Your grace is at work in my life today.

Chapter 47:
Under pressure we don't come unglued

Now I commit you to God and to the word of his grace, which can build you up and give you an inheritance among all those who are sanctified.

Acts 20:32

It is often said that the foundation of a building is its most important part. The depth of the foundation reveals the size and height of the structure the builder has in mind. The taller the building, the deeper the foundation goes. A building built on a weak foundation can buckle under adverse conditions. In the Gospel of Matthew, Jesus gives a parable about two men who built their houses:

Therefore everyone who hears these words of mine and puts them into practice is like a wise man who built his house on the rock. The rain came down, the streams rose, and the winds blew and beat against that house; yet it did not fall, because it had its foundation on the rock. But everyone who hears these words of mine and does not put them into practice is like a foolish man who built his house on sand. The

> *rain came down, the streams rose, and the winds blew and beat against that house, and it fell with a great crash.*
>
> **Matthew 7:24–27**

Both men might have used the same building materials. They might even have built the same type of house. One thing is clear: they built their houses on two different foundations. The wise builder built on the rock, while the foolish builder built on sand. When the storm came, one outlasted the storm but the other fell apart.

Our strength or what we are made up of is usually revealed in the twists and turns of life. Everyone will eventually face a day of trouble or adversity. Solomon says in Proverbs 24:10, 'If you falter in a time of trouble, how small is your strength!' Adversity and trouble are designed to test your strength, which in turn reveals the foundation your life is built on.

The apostle Paul gave a poignant address to the elders of the church at Ephesus. This may well be the last speech he gave before departing to Jerusalem. In his address he leaves them with the Word of God, which is able to build them up and give them an inheritance. The specific word he leaves them with is 'the word of His grace'. God's grace has the ability to build us up and give us an inheritance. This indeed is the right foundation to build our lives on: the word of His grace. This is the rock that holds us together even through the storms of life. Everything else may shake around us, but Christ our sure foundation stays unshakeable. Paul, not knowing what the future had in store for him, was unmoved by the uncertainties of his journey. With a dogged determination to finish his course and testify to the gospel of the grace of God, he persisted. Indeed he ran his race and finished his course because his life was built on the sure foundation of God's grace.

Our strength is determined by our foundation. Our foundation is Christ Jesus the solid Rock. The grace of God is what holds us together. Under pressure we don't come unglued, instead we stay intact. The winds may blow and the waves may roar, but by His grace we will not cower. Your inheritance effortlessly finds its way to you as you are built on the word of His grace.

PRAYER

Heavenly Father, thank You for Your grace. I thank You that the word of Your grace is my foundation. I am built by Your grace and receive all my inheritance effortlessly. Whatever the demands of life are today, I am conscious of the truth that You are my sure foundation.

CHAPTER 48:
WE CAN'T, BUT HE CAN

Jesus, once more deeply moved, came to the tomb. It was a cave with a stone laid across the entrance. "Take away the stone," he said. "But, Lord," said Martha, the sister of the dead man, "by this time there is a bad odour, for he has been there four days." Then Jesus said, "Did I not tell you that if you believe, you will see the glory of God?" So they took away the stone. Then Jesus looked up and said, "Father, I thank you that you have heard me. I knew that you always hear me, but I said this for the benefit of the people standing here, that they may believe that you sent me." When he had said this, Jesus called in a loud voice, "Lazarus, come out!" The dead man came out, his hands and feet wrapped with strips of linen, and a cloth around his face. Jesus said to them, "Take off the grave clothes and let him go."

John 11:38–44

Can you look at or around your life and point to some things you deem to be dead? Are there situations you think could certainly do with a bit of life? Do you sometimes get started on an endeavour with great zest and impetus only to later run dry of the motivation to finish? Maybe there are relationships that you need revived, businesses you need raising up.

Well today, because of Jesus, there is enough power to raise every dead situation.

When Jesus Christ died on the cross, He took our place. When Jesus was raised up from the dead, we were raised up together with Him (Ephesians 2:6), and because we were raised up with Him, wherever He is, there we are. Jesus is now seated at the right hand of the Father. By virtue of position, we are also seated at the right hand of the Father because we are in Jesus.

Jesus was raised from the dead because He put away all of our sins when He died on the cross. The resurrection of Jesus is proof that all our sins were completely paid for. When God raised Jesus from the dead, the power of God in all forms and degrees were exerted on the body of Jesus.

Ephesians 1:19 reveals the different degrees of powers exerted on the body of Jesus when God raised Him from the dead. Paul wrote 'And what is the exceeding greatness of his power toward us who believe, according to the working of his mighty power.'

In this verse alone there are four degrees of power. In the Greek language in which the New Testament is written, the four words used to describe the force exerted on Jesus are *dunamis*, *energeia*, *kratos* and *ischus*. From Dunamis, we get the English word dynamite. It means might, power and God's ability to perform. Energeia means action, productive work or superhuman activity. Kratos means dominion and strength to complete and perfect. Ischus means strength to overcome immediate resistance.

When God raised Jesus from the dead, He released a dynamic ability that brought about a superhuman activity and gave Jesus absolute dominion over death to overcome the grave.

When Christ was crucified, we were crucified with Him. When He was raised from the dead, we were raised up together with Jesus. This means the same power that raised Jesus from the dead is in you.

You are loaded with power. The very day you received Jesus into your life you were endowed with this power.

'Well, that is so good to know, but I don't see any power in my life', you may think. 'What must I do to see this power at work in my life?' You may say, 'I have lots of dead situations that could do with some of this power.' The key to seeing this power at work in your life is to do the same thing Lazarus did before he was raised. He did nothing. The man was dead! Here is the key to releasing the reservoir of power you have been endowed with. Rest! The greatest power of God is manifested in our lives when we do nothing but rest in the finished work of Jesus.[10] The more we rest, the more power is released. Lazarus was dead for four days. In the natural realm, it was impossible for him to experience life again on earth. Yet as he lay helpless in the tomb, God's grace to raise him from the dead was released.

Abraham experienced the same power. Romans 4 describes the condition of his physical body at an old age – as good as dead. This man too was 'dead'! Yet his body was quickened by God and eventually brought forth a son: Isaac. The key to being productive at such a 'dead' age was believing God.

Look at the dead areas of your life. They may be the very places God wants to raise up again. You too can experience the power of God released to every area of your life when you rest and trust His grace. We can't but He can and His grace is sufficient in the area of our weaknesses.

Prayer

Father, I trust You. I depend completely on Your grace, which is sufficient in every situation of my life. I am quickened by Your grace, and I trust in the life-giving power of Your Word, which can bring life to every area of my life.

---

[10] Joseph Prince, *Rest in the power of His resurrection life* (CD Sermon), 31 March 2013. Singapore: Joseph Prince Resources.

Chapter 49:

Where does it itch?

For we do not have a high priest who is unable to empathise with our weaknesses, but we have one who has been tempted in every way, just as we are – yet he did not sin.

Hebrews 4:15

Before you can help anyone, you need to understand them. You will have to assume the seat of the individual and see life through their lens. If your car is broken and you need it fixed, you take it to your local garage. Before they open up the bonnet or go underneath to start fixing it, the mechanic will ask you a series of questions about the car and what the problem is. They might run diagnostics to determine where the fault is. What they are trying to do is assume your seat and see the problem from your perspective before starting work on the car.

A doctor will not prescribe any medication or course of treatment before finding out the problem or cause of an illness. Like the mechanic, they will have you answer a series of questions: how long have you had the symptoms for? Where does it itch? Do you eat normally or have you lost your appetite?

These questions are not asked to frustrate you but to help determine what the malady is and to find an appropriate course of treatment. Doctors put themselves in the shoes of their patient to see where it hurts before recommending what medication to use.

Our Lord Jesus identified with us when He walked on earth. He was not 50 per cent God and 50 per cent human. He was fully God and fully human. By being human, He identified with us as human beings. He was hungry and sometimes rested. He knew the feeling of being rejected because He was rejected by His very own (John 1:11). He knew what it felt like being in a place where the demands seemed more than the supply, such as the feeding of the five thousand with a little boy's dinner. He understood what it meant to lose a loved one to the horrible grip of death, such as Jairus's 12-year-old daughter. For we have a high priest who understands us and our pain. He understands completely what we are going through and identifies with us because He was born as a man yet without sin. However, being God, He not only can feel the feelings of our infirmities, but has the power to deliver us from our predicament. His grace is sufficient to move us from a place of demand to a place where we are amply supplied, as He did in the feeding of the five thousand. He understands our shame, identifies with us, yet he chooses not to condemn us. Instead, as He did to the woman who was caught in the act of adultery, He shows us so much goodness by giving us a gift of no condemnation and then tells us to go and sin no more. He knows what it means to be tired but also has the ability to strengthen us and revive our weary hearts.

Jesus – our Great High Priest – not only sympathises with us but has the power to deliver us from any and every situation the devil throws at us. Instead of shying away from our Lord, let us draw closer to Him in confidence and boldness to find grace and mercy (Hebrews 4:16). Jesus loves it when we come to Him. He won't condemn you. Come just as you are and receive His grace. Let Him love you until you are satisfied with His love and grace.

Prayer

Jesus, You are my Great High Priest. Today I come boldly to Your throne to receive grace and mercy. You know every need and You understand me. I receive Your grace and I am satisfied with Your love.

Chapter 50:

Free grace

For it is by grace you have been saved, through faith—and this is not from yourselves, it is the gift of God—not by works, so that no one can boast.

Ephesians 2:8–9

Some of the most valuable things in life are intangible and unseen. The air we breathe, though unseen, is vital to our existence. The reassuring and affirming words of a boss or supervisor to an employee may carry more weight than a paycheque given at the end of the month. The words, though unseen, carry huge significance.

Paul, in his letter to the church at Corinth, says, 'So we fix our eyes not on what is seen, but on what is unseen, since what is seen is temporary, but what is unseen is eternal' (2 Corinthians 4:18). In this verse, Paul draws a distinction between the seen and unseen realms. God's grace is eternal compared to the temporary troubles we face.

Grace is unearned, unmerited, undeserved favour. God's grace is limitless and inexhaustible. Grace will never come to an end, so much so that in the ages to come, we will still be amazed by grace:

> *in order that in the coming ages he might show the incomparable riches of his grace, expressed in his kindness to us in Christ Jesus.*
> **Ephesians 2:7**

The Amplified Version of the Bible uses the word 'free' to qualify grace:

> *For it is by free grace (God's unmerited favor) that you are saved (delivered from judgment and made partakers of Christ's salvation) through [your] faith. And this [salvation] is not of yourselves [of your own doing, it came not through your own striving], but it is the gift of God*
> **Ephesians 2:8**

Grace is free. If it's not free, it's not grace. There is nothing we can do to earn God's grace. Grace is God's gift given freely to us apart from our performance or merits. Grace, which completely hinges on the great benevolence of God, can never be achieved but only received by believing in the perfect sacrifice of Jesus on the cross of Calvary.

Just because grace is free does not mean it holds no value or is cheap. The freedom we experience as a nation is certainly not cheap freedom. This freedom hinges on the shoulders of those who gave their lives in the fight for our freedom. God's grace is free to the receiver but cost the Giver everything. It cost God everything to give Jesus as a payment for our sins. Grace is not free from the side of the giver, Jesus paid for it. Jesus paid for our salvation so that by believing and not working, we may freely receive all the Father has for us.

If we are saved by free grace, then today we live and enjoy life by free grace. God wants you to rest in what Jesus did for us two thousand years ago. Don't try to earn God's blessing by working for it. Rest in the knowledge that Jesus did it all for you and by faith you have access to all God's blessing.

PRAYER

I am saved by grace, apart from my effort or works. I can do nothing to earn or receive God's grace other than believing. Today, I choose to believe and put my faith in the perfect sacrifice of Jesus. The same grace that saved me 2,000 years ago is the same grace that directs my life today.

Chapter 51:
Perfect Peace

You will keep in perfect peace those whose minds are steadfast, because they trust in you.

Isaiah 26:3

It was the countdown to our baby's due date. With less than two days to go, we just could not wait to receive this perfect gift of God's creation into our family and home. The anticipation of receiving such a blessing into this world was palpable. We could hardly sleep. While the baby was in the womb, He reminded us so much of his big brother Joshua, who was also a highly active baby; one full of beans. Sometimes, you could see the kicks and the shape of his little feet protruding and stretching to the side of his mother's belly.

It was seven in the morning and Joshua had just woken up. "Hey Joshua, let's get your baby brother's cot ready," I said. He was so excited at being involved in setting up his baby brother's bed. "Next," I said, "we need to get the pram and pushchair all ready". It was so much fun putting it all together. Neo his sister also helped round the house with cleaning and preparing for the new arrival. So fast did the day pass and more preparations went into the baby's room. Yes, we were almost there.

The following day, we made our way to see the midwife for a normal routine check-up. "How are you feeling today?" the midwife asked Bakang. "I'm fine," Bakang responded. "I just can't wait any longer for the baby to arrive."

"Well let's have a feel of your tummy and check the baby is OK," said the midwife. So Bakang got on the examination bed and with some gel smeared over her belly, the midwife listened for the heartbeat using a hand-held Doppler.

After almost ten minutes of searching for the heartbeat, she hesitantly said "I'm afraid I can't seem to find the baby's heartbeat. Sometimes it's difficult to find because the baby is ready to be delivered," she continued. "My Doppler may not be picking up any sound but the best thing to do is go to the hospital to make sure everything is ok". She was very supportive. She called the hospital's maternity unit on our behalf and told them to expect us.

We left the midwife and rushed home first to partake of the Holy Communion and pray. We remembered how God had graciously kept the baby and believed He was in control of everything. We were perfectly at rest and not worried. Our hearts were kept in perfect peace. After praying, we dashed to the hospital. On arrival at the maternity unit, we were taken into a room and more tests were conducted by doctors and other professionals to check for the baby's heartbeat. Finally, we got the news we did not expect. "Sorry, there is no heartbeat, your baby has passed away!"

How do you explain the death of a perfectly healthy baby that was carried full term, with no known cause? How do you comprehend the death of a baby only a few hours before it is due to be born? This was a perfect pregnancy with nine months of no complications or illness for either mother or baby. Just a few hours ago, we felt you moving and kicking, and we are now told you are gone?

In John 16:33, Jesus reminded His disciples not to be moved by the tribulations and trials of this world. He said, "I have told you these things, so that in me you may have peace. In this world you will have trouble. But take heart! I have overcome the world."

You may have lost something or someone dear to your heart and are in that place of pain. You may be heartbroken and it may seem that your world is crumbling down. It may be a loved one who has passed away or a lover who has walked away from a thriving relationship. It may be yet another exam that you have failed to pass or a business deal that you've missed out on. Maybe it's an investment in which you've lost all of your life savings or your cat that has just passed away. In the midst of this tragic state, the good news is that you are alive, and to the living there is hope.

Yes, we will not see our baby Joseph Rafiwa Oniye on this side of life, but we are consoled that we know he is right in the presence of our heavenly Father who knows all things. We are comforted to know that God counted on us to carry this baby for almost nine months, and what an awesome privilege that was.

Joseph was delivered two days later. A perfectly beautiful baby boy, with the eyebrow of his mother and the nose of his father. Beautiful in every way, yet without life. We are comforted to know that he has fallen asleep and is with the Lord and we will see him another day. He can't come to us but we will go to him.

Looking around me, I am truly blessed with such a loving and gracious wife, Bakang, and two amazing kids, Neo and Joshua. Most of all I am so blessed because I see God's grace sufficient for me in every way. God is good and perfect in all His ways. God is certainly not the author of death, but we know that even in the midst of tragedy, His grace will shine through and He will make everything beautiful in its time. We are comforted to know the Lord is here with us right now as reiterated in the beautifully written song, Here Now.

> *Here Now, all I know is I know that you are here now, Still my heart let your voice be all I hear now, Spirit breath like the wind come have your way, Cause I know you're in this place.*[11]

---

[11] Here Now (Madness), *Words and Music by* Joel Houston and Michael Guy Chislett, ©2015 Hillsong Music Publishing (APRA) CCLI: 7037919.

Today, be encouraged! You may have lost some things but you have not lost everything. God's grace is still with you and His face is smiling on you. His eyes are forever watching over you. His mercies are new every morning and He still has great plans for your life. Your best days are still ahead. Weeping may endure for a night, but joy always comes in the morning.

Don't languish in the doldrums of depression because of what has happened or hasn't happened yet. Keep trusting in and believing God. He loves you with an everlasting love and His grace is sufficient for you.

PRAYER
Heavenly father, I thank you so much for the gift of life. Before I was formed in my mother's womb, you knew me. You know me so intricately, I am fearfully and wonderfully made. Today, I trust you and rest in your grace that is sufficient for me. Thank you that even right now, all things are working together for my good.

Chapter 52:
Receiving the Call to Grace

For God so loved the world that he gave his one and only Son, that whoever believes in him shall not perish but have eternal life. For God did not send his Son into the world to condemn the world, but to save the world through him.

John 3:16–17

As I kid, I remember writing letters to my parents who were on vacation and sending them a list of things I'd like them to get me. Top of the list were roller skates, apples and chocolates. The letters took about three weeks to be delivered, and we waited another three weeks to hear back. There were no emails, WhatsApp, Facebook or the Internet then. We had access to a telephone but could only use it once a month.

It's great to see the advancement of technology and its impact, especially on the area of communication. Just at the click of a button, an email is sent. Today we cannot only talk to each other from a distance far away, but can also see each other through video messaging. Wow!

Despite the advancement of technology and its impact on society, a few things stay the same: the people, the emotions and the content of messages. Mum is still Mum, ever loving and caring, the emotions are still there to be cherished and shared. The 'I love you Mum and Dad' never ceases, and even as grown ups, we still make requests. It may not be roller skates or apples, but it is still a 'Hi Mum, we're in the area. Can we come over for lunch?'

The message God passed to Adam and Eve in the garden is still the same one He wants you to receive today. Adam and Eve were created and placed in a garden where all they ever needed was already provided, because God took care of them. He showed them His grace and asked them to freely eat of every tree with the exception of one. They didn't need to do anything to qualify for God's goodness except enjoy all that God had already provided for them.

God's message for you is the same today. He has already made a way through the person of Jesus and wants you to know that He is ever loving and ever gracious. He is a good God and wants to take good care of you. Will you let him? The message is 'I love you so much, and have already shown My love to you through Jesus. If you believe and receive Him, you can enjoy all I have prepared for you.'

The call from God today is a call to grace. God does not expect you to come to Him as a perfect person. He wants you just the way you are. You may ask 'What about all the bad things I've ever done?' The answer is that God already knew those deeds before they were done, knows what we are up to today, and knows our future. He knows all about us and yet still longs to have us, just the way we are.

His call is not conditional. It is unconditional. There are no hoops to jump through to experience His goodness. There are no mountains to climb. No oceans to cross or tests to pass before we are accepted by Him. God made you, knows you and wants you. He wants you to come with all your flaws and no pretence. He wants both the person and their flaws. Don't let your flaws hinder you from receiving the call to experience all of God's goodness.

All He requires of us is to dash to the phone as it rings and pick up the call. He wants you to believe His love for you. At our very worst He gave us His very best. He sent Jesus to die for us while we were all sinners. All God desires is that we believe in the gift of His Son Jesus Christ and accept Him into our lives as our Lord and Saviour. Will you receive the call to grace? Will you let Jesus into your heart as your Lord and Saviour?

This is the call to Grace: *God so loved the world that He gave His only begotten Son that whosoever believes in Him shall not perish but have everlasting life.*

SALVATION PRAYER
Dear Jesus, I believe in Your sacrifice for me on the cross of Calvary. I know the Father loves me and because of His love for

me, You died on the cross. You died to pay for all my sins on the cross. Thank You for loving me so much and taking my place on the cross. I receive You into my heart as my Lord and Saviour. I receive Your forgiveness and gift of no condemnation. Today, I receive Your call to grace.

*(If you prayed this prayer for the first time today, you have just made the greatest decision of your life. We want to hear from you. Also if this book has been a blessing to you, please send us an email at **hello@realityofgrace.org**)*

Closing Words

Thank you for taking the time to read and meditate on this book. I hope you have been blessed by the truths of God's Word as seen in the person of Jesus.

God is not an abstract being out there who is uninterested about the daily dealings of your life. He is our Father who wants to be involved in our everyday life. He is not an impersonal being like a picture on a wall or a plate on the table. Just like every good father wants to be involved in their children's life, the Lord Himself wants to be involved in our lives.

My prayer is that you will see Jesus in every detail of your life and fall more and more in love with Him. Remember, God delights when we take the position of child and allow Him to be Father to us. God is well pleased when His Children fall at the feet of Jesus and allow Him to meet all their needs. The Father is delighted when we are completely immersed in the abundant supply of the love of His Son Jesus.

I hope the preoccupation of your life will be in seeing Jesus in every area. Something amazing happens when we fix our eyes on Him. We are changed into His image and we are transformed into His likeness from glory to glory by the spirit of the Lord (2 Corinthians 3:18). This indeed is how you can experience the reality of Grace.

Thank you once again for taking the time to read this book. May you always enjoy the super-abounding peace, joy and favour that our Lord Jesus died to give you.

Blessings,
Bayo Oniye.

Stay Connected with us

Let' stay connected through these social media channels:
Facebook.com/bayo.oniye
Twitter.com/bayooniye
Instagram: @bayooniye
www.realityofgrace.org

www.ingramcontent.com/pod-product-compliance
Lightning Source LLC
Chambersburg PA
CBHW050537300426
44113CB00012B/2141